BOOK ONE

P. A. Wagner, Ph.D.

3rd Coast Books
Houston, Texas
2017

Copyright © 2017 by Paul Wagner

All Rights Reserved

All rights reserved. No part of this book may be reproduced or transmitted in any form or by any means, electronic or mechanical. This includes photocopying or recording by any information storage or retrieval system, without written permission from the publisher.

3rd Coast Books
11111 West Little York Rd., #222
Houston, TX 77041
www.3rdCoastBooks.com

ISBN's
Perfect Binding — 978-1-946743-00-8
eBook/.MOBI — 978-1-946743-01-5
eBook/.ePub — 978-1-946743-02-2

Project Coordinator — Rita Mills
Editor & Collaborator — Faye Walker
Text Design — Kathleen J. Shields
Cover Design — Ken Fraser

Printed in The United States of America

Dedication

I would like to dedicate this book to my son Jason who has learned the lessons of running more miles, making the bed and shining your shoes. Do that and all else will work out.

Table of Contents

Dedication	i
Foreword	iv
Preface	v
Acknowledgements	vii
Introduction	ix

PART I: The Beginning

Chapters

1. The Announcement	1
2. The Separation — It Ain't Over 'Til the Fat Lady Sings?	5
3. The Fight	11
Identifying the Enemy	11
No Fault Divorce	13
Launching a Divorce	15
Just Desserts	16
Putting on the Gloves	16
Finding the Real Enemy	17
The Need to Fight	21
Training for the Big Fight	24
Fighting the Right Fight	28
Choosing a Mercenary	30
Conclusion	32

Dedication

I would like to dedicate this book to my son Jason who has learned the lessons of running more miles, making the bed and shining your shoes. Do that and all else will work out.

Table of Contents

Dedication i
Foreword iv
Preface v
Acknowledgements vii
Introduction ix

PART I: The Beginning

Chapters
1. The Announcement   1
2. The Separation —
   It Ain't Over 'Til the Fat Lady Sings?   5
3. The Fight 11
   Identifying the Enemy 11
   No Fault Divorce 13
   Launching a Divorce 15
   Just Desserts 16
   Putting on the Gloves 16
   Finding the Real Enemy 17
   The Need to Fight 21
   Training for the Big Fight 24
   Fighting the Right Fight 28
   Choosing a Mercenary 30
   Conclusion 32

4. The Furies-Meeting Your Enemies 35
    Guilt 44
    Hate and Anger 49
    Fear 53
    Jealousy 61
    Grief 71
5. The Victory 73

Epilogue — Part I 81

PART II: Post Divorce

Chapters
6. Waxing Philosophical 85
7. From Loneliness to Aloneness 89
    Lessonss to be Learned by the Recently Divorced   98
8. Wonderment 99
    Making Wonderment Happen 103
9. Escaping the Pitfalls 105
    Substance Abuse 106
    Workaholism 110
    Reclusiveness 114
    Promiscuity 115
    A Theory of Flirtation 122
    Summary 152
    Avoid 154
10. Parenting Through Divorce 155

Epilogue — Part II 159
About the Author 161

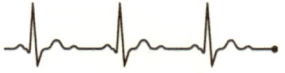

Foreword

This book deals with many personal and sensitive topics as reported by men and women who have experienced divorce. To protect the identity of certain individuals, I have changed names and occupations as necessary. However, when I have done the latter, I substituted occupational descriptions that are as close to the subject's sociocultural and economic role as possible.

When the book deals with women's perceptions or men's perceptions respectively, problems of pronoun reference have been easy to avoid. However, much of what is said affects members of both genders equally. To limit the frequency of "he or she" and "his or her," I used the term *divorcee* as a gender neutral expression. Finally, the title reflects the fact that the concern here is not solely with the traumatizing effects of divorce. There is a "hereafter" following a divorce, a hereafter that every divorcee ultimately strives to make as pleasant as possible. This book is intended to serve as a guide to aid readers in fumbling their way through a divorce and then in making a success of the social life that inevitably follows.

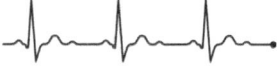

Preface

In sociological and anthropological research there is something called "action research." Action research involves the researcher getting into the midst of what is being studied to get a sense of the phenomenology of it all from the inside out. That is what I have done here.

I have a strong academic background in philosophy and psychology, but, as fate would have it, I was introduced to the world of divorce. Often (but not always as in the case of many medical treatments), the more you know, the more able you are to deal with what is ahead.

I knew nothing about divorce. No one on either side of my family had ever been divorced and even now there has been only one other divorce from the population of two very large extended families now living from coast to coast and even in Australia.

To understand what I was going to be going through, I needed to learn about divorce. To start my investigation, I read a lot. When you know how to read past the whistles and bells and platitudes, there is much to discover. For example, I learned that despite the hype, the divorce rate in this country never once reached the fabled fifty percent erroneously reported on television and in self-help books.

To learn about divorce, I decided I need to learn from those who had been there and from those who were right in the midst of it. Like it or not, I was about to become an action researcher into the phenomenon of divorce.

As I suspected, divorce has a major impact on most people. The impact will differ widely among people. Some, like me, were worried most about what would happen to their children growing up in a broken home. Others worry they may be alone the rest of their lives. Others breathe a sigh of relief to be out of the maelstrom. Others are recklessly eager to get out into the singles' world, expecting to be welcomed by endless numbers of available suitors. It is different for everyone. But the sheer size of the impact seems similar to everyone, and, one way or another, divorce sets up an echo most will hear for the rest of their lives.

In what follows, I want you to hear the voices of those who are living their way through divorce. Along the way, I will share a few academic insights as well, but for the most part this is a book for fellow travelers by fellow travelers.

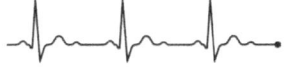

Acknowledgements

To begin, I want to thank the hundreds of people who responded to my very personal and sometimes impertinent questions. In particular, I want to thank the hundreds who shared with me at length the very intimate details of their own divorces. I also want to thank psychologists Zick Rubin and Barbara Herlihy for commenting on the psychological accuracy of the specifically psychological claims made within. Similarly, I want to thank Thomas Stauffer, political scientist and former president of the University of Houston-Clear Lake, for comments pertaining to the analysis of marriage as a political institution.

Also, I want to thank philosophers Richard Grandy, Mitchell Aboulafia, and Thomas Gilbert for their advice on bringing the insights of the great masters to bear on mundane concerns of the present social milieu. I also want to thank the former Reverend Debra Whisnand, senior chaplain of the Southwest Memorial Hospital System, for her comments on the compatibility of the views espoused with current religious views. Former Olympic medalist, author, and running coach Al Lawrence has also made useful comments on the section pertaining to sports as a social arena for singles. Finally, I wish to thank Marco Portales, professor of literature, for his patience in pointing out to me subtleties of language I hope to make this book more readable.

Most especially, considerable thanks is due Vera Fluker, Betty Ann Brott, and Marlene Lewis for their patience and zeal in typing and correcting several earlier drafts of the present volume. Mistakes remaining in the volume are most assuredly my own and were no doubt made despite the expert recommendations of all the above.

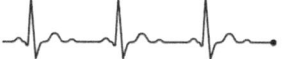

Introduction

One good thing about divorce is not everyone has to go through it. Another is most people avoid it. In the majority of cases where divorce is not avoided, things probably could be worked out. For one reason or another, however, many people no longer choose to make the effort. Unlike marriage, which requires two willing partners, divorce requires only one. If a spouse wants a divorce, there is not much the mate can do about it. The marriage is history. This book is not about divorce, nor is it about marriage. Rather this book is about survival in the wake of divorce.

Since the days of Henry the Eighth, divorce has been a well-known phenomenon in the Western World. Indeed, even earlier Biblical writings and other ancient texts indicate the history of divorce, the dissolving of marriages, dates back at least to the time of the early tribal Jews. Since the 1960s, divorce has not only become more frequent but also has come under considerable study by psychologists and other social scientists. The divorced have little need for another book describing studies detailing the causes and effects of divorce. On the other hand, the divorced do need a systematic study of the folk wisdom neighbors share with neighbors, friends with friends, to help them through divorce. This shared folk wisdom is often the most valuable advice one can get. And it does not require scheduled appointments at one hundred and fifty dollars an hour.

The accounts of divorce offered within are filtered through the eyes of those who experienced it, especially those who afterward discovered happiness in their lives. The happiness referred to is not the glee one expresses because he or she is "free," "more in touch with herself," or "like, you know, I feel I've really grown as a result of all this... for sure." Rather, it is the happiness resulting from rejuvenated curiosity. For example, in my own case, I now look at myself and other divorcees with a sense of wonder and delight. There is so much to learn. Until people confront crises such as death, drugs, war, or divorce they can remain oblivious to their sometimes heroic and sometimes cowardly efforts toward achieving success. The divorcee is forced to look at him or herself in new ways. This is a painful process. Nevertheless, for those who complete the process, the rewards are great.

Both through my own personal experience and by interviewing nearly twelve hundred other divorcees, I learned a number of interesting solutions for addressing and getting through the discomfort of post-divorce life. I have summed up these solutions in each chapter in Part I. Each summary details the ways ordinary people learned to put divorce in the past.

I do not wish to pretend the categories I offer are so detailed or refined or so rigorous that behavioral scientists can use them for scientific research. I think behavioral and social scientists will find the book raises provocative issues for further study, but I am happy to leave such study to the appropriate scientists. This is a book by and about ordinary persons. It is addressed to the person who is recently divorced and in search of signposts to both the pitfalls against, and the opportunities for, moving on.

In compiling evidence for this book, I began asking friends and dates questions: what did they think caused their divorce; and what is the function of single life? From their responses, I discovered there are many parallels among seemingly diverse sorts of people. With my interest piqued, for four years I took every opportunity to interview divorcees further on these matters. For the most part, I used no questionnaires or standardized research protocols (occasions when I did are noted in the text).

Rather, I allowed people to tell me their own stories and present their own world views in the most casual and informal manner possible. What I wanted was folk wisdom. I needed to let folks tell their own stories in their own way.

The people I interviewed are middle- and upper-class. Most were white although I did talk with some Blacks and Hispanics as well. Their stories were similar to their socioeconomic counterparts. This leads me to believe divorce is largely unaffected by race or ethnic background. Nevertheless, I believe it is only fair to alert readers to some of the limitations of my research efforts early on.

My sources are limited to people I felt would communicate their deepest and most private thoughts. I did not talk to every person about every topic discussed in this book. I spoke with a person only as long as a given topic sustained the person's interest. All in all, I spoke to well over a thousand people from Boston, Massachusetts; Chicago, Illinois; Columbia, Missouri; Dallas, Texas; Des Moines, Iowa; Fayetteville, Arkansas; Los Angeles, California; New Orleans, Louisiana; New York, New York; Pittsburgh, Pennsylvania; Phoenix, Arizona; San Francisco, California; San Diego, California; Tucson, Arizona; Washington, D.C., and Houston, Texas. Along the way, I also spoke to hundreds of others I met in the above cities but who lived most of their lives somewhere else.

George Gallup and Louis Harris would have gone about this study differently. My models in pursuing this investigation are not the scientific pollsters but skilled social observers like Montaigne, Gail Sheehey, Studs Terkel, and the philosophers Aristotle and Ludwig Wittgenstein. I wanted to learn what principles people believe successfully led them through the most difficult aspects of divorce. Furthermore, as noted above, I wanted to collect and systematize folk wisdom in a way that makes it less ambiguous and more immediately available to the reader.

Not all readers have equally wise neighbors, friends or confidants. Not all readers have the time or money to travel the country ferreting out the recurring themes of problem-solving and useful folk wisdom. I have attempted to make this wisdom available to the reader in a compact, usable form. As a professional philosopher, I have also added some of my own insights while constructing a single, coherent document, a primer for the divorced.

Today is the first day of the rest of your life. In the next few pages, you can find something that will show you what YOU can do today to create a wonderful tomorrow.

LOVE TRAUMA

[Separation to Post Divorce]

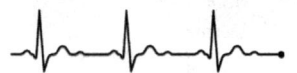

PART I

The Beginning

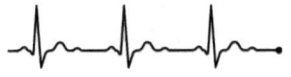

1

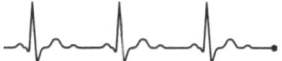

The Announcement — It Only Takes One

Honey, I'm sorry. You're a wonderful person, you're great with the kids, but I just don't love you anymore. I've found someone else. I want a divorce.

You're drunk again. You stay out all night. I don't know who you're with. You spend our money on who knows what. And you get violent with the kids when you're drunk. It's like you have a Jekyll and Hyde personality. I am leaving you. I want a divorce.

It should have been easy to write this chapter. The two examples above were once characteristic of what brings a marriage to its knees. To imagine the divorce scenario, there seemed little else to do but allude to such examples, but much has changed since the time when the divorce scenario was so predictable.

Allan Bloom, the author of *The Closing of the American Mind*, fears feminism and free love are leading to the demise of the family. Christopher Lasch, in *The Age of Narcissism*, blames the baby boomers for their single-minded selfishness. They are, he says, the me-generation. Whatever causes weaker family ties, people base their decisions to divorce on feelings and events much more diverse than they did, say, two generations ago. A novelty country and western song "Yuppie Love," produced in the early 1980s, captures it all. Roughly, the message of the song is if a person believes he or she is no longer benefitting from a "relationship," then it is time to call it quits. Surely, there is more in the minds of those who initiate divorce than is revealed by this blatantly selfish and egocentric profile. To the person being divorced, however, it feels brutal and cold.

Actually, the person initiating the divorce probably does not understand fully why he or she is divorcing the once perceived soulmate. Many of the problems the initiator will confront as a single person far outweigh what the person is currently enduring as a married person. As Eileen, a divorced mother of three observed, "Before I divorced I used to lament the happiness I thought I must be missing. Now, the mere absence of happiness would seem a blessing in contrast to my current struggles just to survive!"

Eileen's warning is bound to fall on deaf ears for persons whose minds are already set on divorce. The lure of freedom and independence strikes the prospective divorcee as more attractive than the challenge of marriage. Furthermore, since divorce seems so common and less objectionable now than it once seemed, persons considering divorce may give little thought to what it means to be a divorcee. The media often portray divorce as a cure for boredom, frustration and anxiety. The message seems to be, "If you are not happy in your marriage, get out and start over."

Most divorcees find starting over is not as easy or pleasurable as they naively hoped it would be. With the announcement the marriage is at an end, a couple confronts two difficult tasks. First, each negotiates the psychological, legal, and financial entanglements of the divorce proceedings. Second, each must learn to see self *as a single person*. For many, the prospect is frightening. They feel being alone is akin to *perpetual loneliness*.

This is not to say divorce can, or should, be avoided at all costs. Sometimes the physical safety of one or both partners makes divorce necessary. Other times, one partner may simply decide to run from the relationship. In either case, while it is true it takes two people to agree to a marriage, it only takes one to initiate a divorce. This means that for some people, regardless of how committed they are to the institution of marriage, they have no choice in their marital future. They are forced to become divorcees. This loss of control over one's immediate future radically disrupts the victim's lifestyle.

Things to Do

1. Read on. You have much to learn. The more quickly you learn it, the better off you'll be.
2. Brace yourself. The process you are about to begin cannot be completed in a few days or a few weeks even. Set your sights on making it through the long haul.
3. Be patient. Don't rush through this book. Make sure you FEEL comfortable with what is being said before you move on.
4. Make friends with several people who seem to you to be successfully coping with divorce.

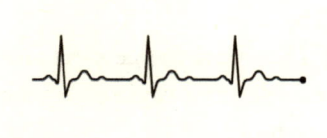

2

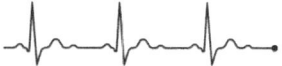

The Separation — It Ain't Over 'Til the Fat Lady Sings?

Once a partner abandons the home, the separation begins. Not all separations are permanent. Some people live apart for anywhere from a couple of weeks to a couple of years and then reunite. There are couples who separated, completed the divorce proceeding, and several years later, remarried. These, however, are extraordinary exceptions, and no one who is divorced or divorcing is advised to hold out hope for a reconciliation.

Still, everyone has heard one or more stories of couples who separated, intending to get divorced, and then reunited a few days or even months later. One particularly intriguing incident was related to me by a divorce attorney. It seems a couple, both in their early thirties, with no children and a rather modest estate, set out to divorce. For months, neither party directly communicated with the other. The hostility between the two was so intense they were constantly calling upon their respective attorneys to convey messages across the battle lines. As is often the case, the attorneys' fees mounted and the estate was reduced. Finally, the two agreed to a settlement and the disputants met in the attorney's office to sign the final papers. The man and woman remained quiet as the lawyers reiterated the conditions of settlement. When all was said, and seemingly done, the lawyers asked their clients to sign the petition and other documents. Both simply sat there. Neither showed any sign of emotion. Everyone waited in silence. After several minutes, the man asked his estranged wife if she wanted a divorce. She said no. With that, the two got up, thanked their lawyers, and walked out. They seemed happy though there was no great outpouring of emotion. They were resolved to stay together, at least for the time being.

Recollection of stories such as this provide hope, often too much hope, for at least one member of an estranged couple. Years later, when looking back at this period in their lives, many people describe it as living through a "fog of anguish." One fifty-ish, accomplished career woman said:

> It all seemed as if I were in a dream or living my life through some kind of fog. I thought I was managing everything quite nicely: career, family, my own place...but I was so lonely. I began drinking at nights—something I had never done before. Finally, about a year later and after a medical crisis, I just stopped and decided to turn my life around... Up to that point I really hadn't taken control of my life. I just lived through a daze.

When she was asked what kept her so remote from reality during this period she said:

> I don't know. I couldn't believe this was happening to me. We had raised a family together. We had been married for over twenty years. I thought divorce only happened to younger people or people

who hadn't really been married that long. You know, people who never really learned what marriage was all about. I thought we knew those things. I guess I thought this was all some kind of bad dream. Or you know what I really thought? I guess "hoped" would be a better word. I hoped that we would get back together. After all, it happened to other people. We had something special—it just couldn't end this way. Anyway, when I look back on it all now, I'm amazed I ever lived through it.

This tragic story of months lost is not unique. A number of men divorced by their wives had similar stories. One does not have to be married for twenty or more years or divorce at the advent of your golden years to become overwhelmed by a torturous mix of grief and hope. The longing for a loved one, for a relationship not yet lost ("It's not over until the fat lady sings," as Don Meredith used to remind viewers on Monday night football), tears at the psychic flesh of the divorcee until he or she accepts it as a *fait accompli*. Everyone to whom I spoke admitted the period of waiting for the final judgment forces one to reflect upon the possibility that some grave error has been made. Many obsess over how to put things back together again. Most veterans of this experience conclude these moments of doubt are inevitable psychological concomitants of the divorce process. Unfortunately, like Humpty Dumpty, once a marriage is broken, not even all the king's men can put it together again. Still, is it really broken...?

No doubt many have wondered why it takes so long to get a divorce. Surely, if it took less time to get a divorce, much ambivalence and anxiety could be avoided. Should the length of time it takes to get a divorce be shortened? In many states, it now takes only sixty days to get a divorce and another thirty to be free to re-marry. If people want a divorce, why shouldn't they be able to get one when they want it? Why does the law require people to endure the torment of legal separation prior to divorce?

The obvious reasons are of a strictly business nature. Some adults see marriage and divorce as little more than going together and breaking up. It is not only the Zsa Zsa Gabors, Larry Kings and Elizabeth Taylors who have passed through marriage a multiplicity of times. A number of ordinary Americans, their dreams full of life in the fast lane, stumble through relationships always in search of an unachievable high. If these people were truly free to make and break relationships at their whim, one can easily imagine the difficulty it would cause creditors trying to recover payment on the couple's debts. Besides business matters, the State feels it has an interest in preserving the family as a social institution. For many Americans, the nuclear or extended families in which they grew up no longer seem like viable options. On the other hand, an amazing number of people who went through their twenties and thirties in quest of the next big thrill, the next big achievement, now seem to long for the family experience they remember as a child. The Cleaver family of *Leave it to Beaver* fame is much maligned now when people talk about relationships in public. A growing number of people, however, privately harbor a desire for the sort of unquestioned reciprocal commitment the Cleavers apparently enjoyed.

In any case, the law has long supported marriage and the family as institutions meriting protection. Philosophers, legal theorists, social theorists, and practicing jurists are all quick to note strong family ties strengthen the stability of a community. Divorce creates instability. Instability is the enemy of community.

Children are common casualties of the instability divorce creates. For example, studies show children of divorced parents are more likely to become divorced themselves thus guaranteeing a cascading proliferation of divorce-caused instability for generations to come. In addition, children often suffer academic difficulties shortly following their parents' divorce. This reflects the disruptive effects of divorce on the children's natural development. Finally, parents, relatives, neighbors, and friends often find themselves drawn into hostile entanglements with warring divorcees. Small subcommunities become embroiled in conflict created by the divorce of one couple. In short, divorce sets off waves of difficulty for many others besides the estranged husband and wife. There should be no surprise, then, the courts see sustaining the institution of marriage and protecting the public from its failure as in the community's best interest.

  Since this book is meant to be a guide to life after divorce, I will not attempt to justify the court's reasoning on this issue. Suffice it to say divorce is often inevitable and the separation leading to divorce is, for most, the first step toward a new life as a divorcee. Presumably, those who find reason to re-unite during this period are fortunate and have no need for what is to follow. However, for others what really matters is "How do I make it through divorce and beyond?"

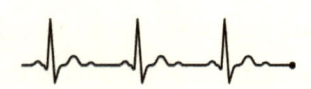

3

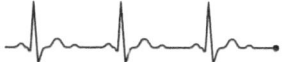

The Fight — Finding the Enemy

Cordial divorces are rare although they may occur when there is little property to divide or custody considerations to settle. In most cases, divorce involves a fight. The fight may be large-scale warfare, bitter and enduring, or it may be no more than a guerrilla action, a series of skirmishes where bruised feelings seek release.

Divorce fights are peculiar. They are not the eyeball to eyeball one ordinarily imagines when conjuring up the scene of a fight. People feel the first question they must address is whether they should fight the divorce. A divorce is a legal action and, properly speaking, can be contested, but it cannot be fought. A fight is an interpersonal affair, so when people fight they must fight some *one* and not some *thing*. But who should be fought in a divorce?

Identifying the Enemy

The most likely candidate for attack is the spouse. But what if you still love your spouse? How do you fight someone you love, cherish, and adore? How do you fight someone with whom you have been sharing your life through sickness and in health until, you thought, death and death alone set you apart? How do you fight someone who is dear to you? Typically, you don't. You tend to look for other targets.

If your estranged spouse has a lover, that person appears to be the perfect target. But how do you fight your spouse's lover? Do you point out how awful the person is? Do you insist to your spouse you are so much better than the competition? Whatever you choose to do, the divorce proceeds afoot. You gain nothing by attacking your spouse's lover other than to subject yourself to further humiliation and rejection.

What about your spouse's friends? Did they poison the well? Suppose you tell your spouse they contaminated your marriage with their nasty tales and self-serving criticisms. This may or may not be true. If your spouse is surrounded by people who have little respect for marriage, he or she is likely to develop a distaste for your relationship. People of the same sex with little esteem for marriage tend to encourage associates to neglect or reject the demands of matrimony. Those who de-value marriage tend to be quick to make disparaging remarks about marriage and the opposite gender. People of the opposite gender with little respect for the institution feel free to encroach upon other marriages by flirting and making sexual advances. The impending dissolution of your marriage may well be a consequence of the intrusions of others. Yet once your spouse decides to dissolve the marriage, it is too late; the damage has already been done.

One off-handed remark or one atypical flirtation does not ordinarily dissuade a person from matrimonial commitment. Over time, what a person experiences routinely tends, inevitably, to shape him or her. This is not to say people are simply a function of their experience but rather to recognize experiences have a cumulative effect in forming people's responses to future stimuli. For example, the most arrogant of male and female narcissists often boast, "We just grew apart" or more typically, "I grew and he/she didn't." Such views reflect an obliviousness to the fact this couple once undertook a *common life project*. If one grows, why can't that person help the spouse grow? Is that not part and parcel of undertaking a marriage relationship? While the narcissist aptly recognizes his or her experiences and subsequent attitudes changed the relationship, the narcissist fails to recognize that each spouse willingly and conjointly undertook the common project of joining their lives. Each had the responsibility of helping the other develop in the accumulation of new *shared experiences*. New growth-provoking experiences, when conscientiously shared between people, sustain the love of marriage and help it grow. It is the *failure to share* which leads to disparate levels of growth.

Disparate growth between partners occurs when each spouse pursues an individual agenda—-an agenda in which the other is, at best, invited to accompany the spouse on fewer and fewer occasions. Nevertheless, the divorcee must still face the fact that once great disparities occur, there is no turning back. How things evolved or how they got out of hand is no longer an important question. All that matters now is the bond of wedlock is broken and plans must be made to ensure all parties survive.

No Fault Divorce

The spouse who, over months and years, has become estranged *is* now a different person. There is no way to turn back the clock—certainly not by attacking the spouse's friends or lover. At times, a traumatic event over which neither husband nor wife had any control can destroy a marriage. Such things as substance abuse, rape, or the abduction, death, or serious illness of a child may each create such mental and psychological turmoil in the life of a couple that they no longer know how to go on together. Such marriages perhaps could have been saved through appropriate and timely counseling, but counseling often is no longer an option once the adversarial proceedings of divorce begin. How does one fight a rape, an illness, or an abduction? One does not.

Perhaps fighting is not what divorce should be about. Why can't people be civilized about such things? They can't because they are in the process of rejecting one another and rejection hurts. If the couple cooperated on major projects in the first place, they would not now be divorcing. When one looks into the few well-mannered divorces one encounters, it often becomes apparent neither partner had much affection for the other—hence, it was easy to be "civilized." In other cases, one partner feels lovingly towards the spouse or is so over-wrought with guilt he or she does not feel justified in fighting back. And the mate who carries a torch or suffers residual guilt is usually easy to spot. The final divorce decree confirms these conclusions. Sharp imbalances in the division of goods, for instance, typically reveal not the skill of lawyers but rather the failure of one party who could not or would not fight for a more equitable distribution of community resources.

The amount of guilt one feels may have little or nothing to do with the wrongs one did or did not commit. Although the appropriateness of guilt may be rationally assessed by an objective observer, no participant in the divorce qualifies as an objective observer. More important, it is not at all clear at this point that assessment of guilt really matters or is resolvable. Regardless of merit, regardless of apparent decorum, guilt mutilates both people.

If you cannot fight the spouse's lover, friends, or tragic event, whom, or what, do you fight? Eventually people find love is not terribly far from hate. The very person you never wanted to be without becomes the person you never again want to see. At this point, the object of attack becomes your estranged spouse. In other cases, a competent lawyer must drag the lovelorn defendant, kicking and screaming, to fight for property, and, when children are involved, child support, custody or favorable visitation rights. In each case, *it looks as if* the target of attack should be your former marriage partner.

Launching the Divorce

Given these views, the reader may think I am committed to viewing divorce as an arena for combat. In fact, divorce is an adversarial proceeding. People contest the other's right to jointly acquired goods and to the custody of their children. Divorce is not about friendship, cooperation, or community interests. Marriage is, divorce is not. Divorce is not meant to promote enduring friendship among equals. One spouse may ostensibly befriend the other while spiriting away the material goods of the union. That hardly counts as friendship. Divorce is simply not the sort of social fabric weaved from goodwill. During my divorce, I talked with one amiable middle-aged man who made this point startlingly clear to me. He was forty-eight years old, accomplished, friendly, and kind to everyone he met. He seemed to be a "hail fellow well-met" who had found Nirvana on earth. He had been divorced from his wife for over a decade. We chatted briefly about my divorce. Instead of consoling me about the impending divorce, he laughed and said, "Just remember as you go through this, your friend doesn't divorce you!"

Détente may be the fairest and most reasonable substitute for contrived efforts to be friendly. Under conditions of détente, opponents reach agreements in a cautious, deliberate and self-restrained way. They strike deals rather than attack an enemy.

Just Desserts

When my divorce began, I immersed myself in self-pity and guilt. I felt guilty since surely no one divorces you unless you "deserve it." This, it turns out, is a common belief for many divorcees to hold. The person being sued for divorce feels he or she must somehow deserve it though, in more than a few cases, there exists no rational grounds for this belief. There may be actions and deeds one ought to feel guilty about, but guilt and divorce are not synonymous or even causally-related concepts. Divorce is seldom based on someone's merit or lack of such. A person does not divorce a spouse because the spouse "deserves" it. Individuals seek divorce because they need to or at least think they need to.

Putting on the Gloves

All right, so a divorce requires a fight. How should the fight take place? And who or what should be attacked? The first thing to remember at this point is in a few months you will be living the rest of your life as a divorced person. Once the fight begins, there is little hope for recovering the marriage. How you fight will likely determine the quality of your life after the divorce and perhaps even the length of your life. Be careful not to waste energy charging at windmills or becoming a scoundrel. Falling victim to either pattern involves considerable psychological and physical risk. Take time and think through the consequences of your proposed activities.

Finding the Real Enemy

Researchers report there is substantial risk of suffering a morbid event within the first year following a divorce. For some reason, the risk is much greater for men than for women. I have heard women chauvinists speculate this is because marriage is an institution designed to tax women for the benefit of men. According to this view, when men are deprived of marriage, they simply fall apart. In contrast, women often discover for the first time in their lives divorce frees them from the burden of male dominance or dependence.

Male chauvinists believe men typically put much more into marriage than women and so when marriages dissolve, men suffer a greater sense of loss than women. Male chauvinists might well turn to feminist psychologists like Carol Gilligan for grist to support the claim that men's greater sense of loss following a divorce is evidence of greater commitment to marriage. Gilligan's research suggests women are much better at establishing friendships than men. Men may play poker or golf with "the boys" or racquetball or tennis with a friend, but they do not develop much intimacy in these relationships. The activities men enjoy promote competition, not cooperation. Women tend to build strong and more intimate relationships with other women than men do with men. Women typically engage in activities focusing on sustaining cooperative relationships with their peers, Gilligan explains. Women's clubs and activities invite the sharing of intimacy whereas male competition prevents bonding and opportunities for sharing intimacy. If this is so, then perhaps the reason men are more likely to suffer from divorce is marriage is their one source of intimate contact. When men are deprived of marriage, they feel they have lost all intimacy.

The psychological literature leaves little doubt: when people feel they have lost all opportunity for intimacy, their ability to deal with stress decreases dramatically. This, in turn, leads to increased incidence of suicide, cancer, high blood pressure, and heart disease. If men have restricted their expression of intimacy to the family alone, then it is no surprise divorce leads them to believe they have no other reservoir of intimate relationships to which they can turn for support. At these times, they become most vividly and painfully aware the old adage "No man is an island" is true. The total loss of intimacy brings severe grief, and this leads to other self-destructive tendencies in men. Let me hasten to add there is no more scientific evidence for this account of the higher morbidity rate among post-divorce males than for the account given by female chauvinists.

Surely one reason males suffer higher morbidity following divorce is their disproportionate propensity for alcohol consumption. Both men and women can be victimized by alcoholism following a divorce. But according to government statistics, the prevalence of alcohol consumption among males compared to females is higher at all ages, income bracket and marital status. It's not surprising, then, recently divorced men are more likely to succumb to alcohol-related problems than are women. This fact alone explains some of the difference in post-divorce morbidity patterns between the sexes, but not all. The dramatic disproportion in numbers leaves much unexplained and deserving of further research.

Regardless of how one chooses to interpret the data, morbidity tables underscore the intensity of stress in divorce. Viciously fighting out a divorce produces little satisfaction, and it may increase a person's chance for serious illness or worse. If divorce makes a fight inevitable, then it is an advantage to fight in such a way the divorcee can live to tell about it!

From the perspective of life after divorce, there is only one way to fight: *you must fight honorably*. If ever there was a place for a Geneva Accord or a Marquis of Queensbury Rules of Pugilism, divorce is the place. People who become ruthless during divorce psychologically maim other people as well as themselves. Despite all temptation to the contrary, the divorcee must fight back *with honor*. To know always what it means to fight with honor can be difficult. Where does fighting with honor begin? Where does fighting with honor end and being over-wrought with guilt begin? The following account illustrates how difficult it is to address this question.

A thirty-eight-year old educational consultant, Tony, explained when his divorce began, he was willing to give his wife everything. He knew she was a good person. She wanted the kids and the means to take care of them. She also wanted him out of her life. This man did not drink, chase women, use drugs, and he abused neither his wife nor his children. He made a comfortable income which, when matched with his wife's, provided the family a pleasant lifestyle. When I asked him why he felt compelled to give his wife everything she requested, he wandered his way through a number of half-believable reasons. He wanted the kids well cared for. (He also thought he could do a good job of it himself, but that did not seem to matter. He apparently felt he did not deserve to have them.) He thought he owed his wife. When asked if he had ever seriously wronged his wife, neglected, or abused her, he said, "No." Ultimately, he said, "She had remained trim and pretty while I got fat and ugly." Maybe this was the cause of the divorce. Maybe he should have felt ashamed for not taking better care of himself. But it is not as if he set out to hurt someone. He did not deserve to punish himself, nor did he deserve punishment from anyone else.

Reason is not what motivates people at the time of divorce. For this man, divorce was the punishment he deserved. He was guilty as charged. For five days, he didn't sleep and ate very little. Finally, he decided he had to do something to survive. He went out and jogged three miles. That night, he finally slept. He continued running each day, and he started eating fruits and vegetables. Eventually, he felt strong enough to confide in a friend his wife was divorcing him. His friend was a wise, elderly woman. A person who had seen many divorces and had counseled one of her own children through divorce, the woman urged him to fight back. He did.

His wife had said he could take anything from the house he wished but at the end of two weeks, she would lock the doors. Up to that point, he had taken only a mattress, some books, clothes, a clock, and a meager assortment of old tableware. After deciding he must fight, he went back to the house and retrieved box after box of his mother's china, crystal and silverware. These he returned to his mother. His intention was not to deprive his wife or children of anything nor was it to enrich himself in any way. He was simply taking his first step toward recovery. He was fighting back. He did no harm to anyone. His wife never objected to his taking the heirlooms—though she did not volunteer he get them, either. The value of his action was he abandoned the role of passive bystander. He had taken control of his destiny and was now an active participant in his own divorce.

Whether at the time he realized it or not, this man not only began the invaluable task of fighting back, but he sensed the appropriate target. In a divorce, when you meet the enemy you may be surprised to find out it is you, yourself. You are the one most likely to mismanage your divorce. You are the one who will regret any show of vengeance or maliciousness when the divorce is over. You are the one who will lose respect for yourself if you look back on the divorce and realize you were cowardly, spiritless, or a mere pawn in the hands of others.

The Need to Fight

Fighting back in a divorce is a matter of *preserving* self-respect. Fighting back *with honor* is a matter of *enhancing* self-respect. To fight back with honor requires you objectify your relationship with the other disputant. The philosopher Thomas Nagel in his book *The View From Nowhere* notes apprehending absolute truth is well beyond the means of any individual. Nevertheless, says Nagel, we can increase our understanding of a situation by stepping outside ourselves, as it were, and examining as best we can our own role in that situation as though it might be that of any other participant. Translated to the context of divorce, Nagel's recommendation amounts to this: if you were told about the elements of a divorce identical to your own, upon reflection, you would insist on what is minimally due each participant. By looking at your own divorce in this manner, you would recognize there is some division of goods which denies no one his or her minimal rights. In other words, you must guard against taking advantage of your spouse. And, similarly, you should be no more and no less protective of yourself than you are of your estranged spouse. Each disputant in a divorce is worthy of equal respect. This is not to say each is equally worthy of affection or an equal division of goods. But each is worthy of the full complement of just treatment our society tries to reserve for all.

After you secure what is minimally due each litigant, how do you ensure the divorce settlement is optimally just? You don't. This is practically impossible to achieve and is the sort of detail work best left to lawyers. Even if you follow Nagel's advice and view the situation as if you were not involved, you cannot wholly pull off this "God's eye" view. Particularly in the case of an emotion-packed experience such as divorce, intelligent, well-meaning and thoughtful people cannot help but skew their respective pictures of the optimal divorce settlement. You have done all you can when you ensure neither of you is being taken advantage of by the other or by an enterprising lawyer. Beyond that, if your spouse ends up getting a bit more than is deserved—what of it?

As Plato reminds us, who suffers the greater injury, the person who is wronged or the person who wrongs another? The first is victimized and no doubt suffers as a result. However, if the person's victimization reflects no gross self-neglect or abuse, then the person's character and honor remain intact, and these are the most self-defining features we possess. The second person dishonors self by inflicting wrongful injury on another and thus lives a disreputable life, displaying a tarnished sense of honor. His or her character is flawed forever more. Plato's stoicism may sound a bit Pollyanna-ish to the modern ear, but it is not. Even a person influenced by the moral nihilism of Ayn Rand will have to agree there may be good reason to err more on the side of sustaining *slight injury* than intentionally inflicting injury of any kind on another. The former preserves one's sense of dignity; the latter erodes it.

Apparently, human nature being what it is, people possess what the eighteenth-century philosopher David Hume calls "a sense of social sympathy." Acts of injustice offend people while acts of benevolence exhilarate them. Yet people can, and do, act contrary to their sense of social sympathy. However, when they do, they experience guilt. The emotion of guilt and its relation to wrongdoing has been studied extensively from the time of Immanuel Kant, in the eighteenth century, to the present work of psychiatrist Karl Menninger of the famed Menninger Institute. Psychologically normal people who do wrong experience guilt. The intensity of the guilt seems somehow proportionate to the perpetrator's sense of the crime. If you act in a petty and malicious way during your divorce, you live with the perception of yourself as petty and malicious for some time afterward. The more grievous and frequent your misdeeds, the longer you will suffer guilt.

Psychologists report it typically takes anywhere from two years to half the length of time one was married to recover from a divorce. Thus, the divorcee can expect to dwell on any and all wrongdoing incurred during a divorce for a considerable length of time. If you are self-interested and want to recover from divorce as rapidly as possible, be careful to avoid intentional wrongdoing during the divorce proceedings. When your spouse is long gone and you have only yourself to live with, you are very much going to want to like yourself. It is difficult to like yourself if you disrespect yourself.

Remember, the most vicious enemy you will confront in a divorce is yourself. If you fight back with honor, you will do much to prepare the way for a timely and successful post-divorce recovery.

The first urge many people experience upon entering the divorce process is to give up the fight to survive. They spend all their waking hours either ruminating spitefully about people and events in the past or dreading what looks like an empty, joyless future. Each of these responses is a consequence of an attack by the furies (see Chapter Four). You can let the furies run rampant and lose control over your life. Or you can put your life under strict control. The more control you exercise over your activities, the more quickly your attitudes and moods will change and the more quickly you will learn to enjoy life.

Training for the Big Fight

"Getting control over your life" is a curious notion.

Literally speaking, if you do not control your life, who else can? Clinical and counseling psychologists use this phrase with abandon while many philosophers and scientific-types find the expression meaningless. Strictly speaking, when I make a decision or engage in some action it is *my brain,* and no one else's, sending messages to the relevant muscles and nerve endings. No one can *think* for me any more than they can *feel* my grief or my fatigue. No voluntary action can be undertaken by me without something occurring within my physiology. So what does it mean to say, "You must get control over yourself"? How can it be that your self can act outside your control?

These questions tantalize philosophers, annoy self-help gurus, and confuse laypersons. Rather than belabor the issue in any philosophic or scientific way, I will address the issue from the perspective of "lived experience," the experience of those who have successfully fought their way through divorce.

To begin with, always remember a fight is a fight. No matter how nobly one engages in a fight, it will be taxing both physically and psychologically. To meet the challenge of a divorce fight, you must get into good physical shape as quickly as your body allows. Getting into good physical shape will accomplish two things.

First, it will give you the stamina and strength to endure some difficult and heart-wrenching proceedings. Second, it will benefit you psychologically by giving you a feeling of greater self-control. Because you are likely to find you are your own worst enemy during a divorce, you are the one who may act in such a way and, years after the divorce, you will feel regret for any scandalous behavior. Most of the reprehensible, disdainful behavior occurring during a divorce happens because a person loses control over emotions. Wrecked emotional states wreak havoc through people's actions. If you lose control, you are likely to respond to each subsequent misdeed with more confusion and even more intense emotion.

Each misdeed costs you self-esteem. With each loss of self-esteem, a person becomes more desperate to regain what is lost. This desperation leads to further misdeeds until eventually the person hits rock bottom where the loss of self-esteem is complete. To avoid this eventuality, keep in mind your ultimate goal should be to ensure an expeditious post-divorce recovery. Throughout all the proceedings, fight to maintain control over yourself. With control, you will preserve your self-esteem.

Shortly after my own divorce began, I commiserated with several people. I learned divorcees are quick to share their experiences with other divorcees. The folk wisdom on how to handle "the fight" is readily available—just ask any old-timer at divorce how he or she managed "the fight." The key to success is nearly always the same. "Get control over your life… NOW." Most divorcees sheepishly admit their quest to regain control over their lives followed a troubled and circuitous route. But once control is restored, they begin to recover.

Consider this story of a forty-ish university administrator. He had been a tee-totaler all his life. After being divorced by a woman to whom he had been married for five years, he became a recluse and sought solace through overindulgence in alcohol. A year later, he developed medical problems. In response to his doctor's stern warning, he went on the wagon. Without the distraction of alcohol, he gradually regained a sense of control over his destiny. He ventured out on a date or two and eventually resumed a stable life-style. In three years, he became engaged to a lovely woman his own age, and the two of them are now quite happy.

He felt he had no control over his life and, as a consequence, he lost further control by turning to the bottle. However, once he became conscientious and objective about making decisions reflecting his own best interest, his life became more satisfying. (Recall Nagel's prescription for gaining an objective view of life.)

A thirty-one-year old woman, Sally, who still had the figure and bounce of her high school cheerleading days told me:

> My first husband cheated on me. I couldn't take it, so I moved into an apartment and divorced

him. Even though I divorced him, I felt that I was the one who was being rejected. I even let him take all our property. Why did he run around on me? What was wrong with me? There was a guy across the hall from me in the new apartment building; he was nice to me throughout the divorce. Normally, I wouldn't have talked to him. He smoked, drank, had long hair, and drove a Harley-Davidson motorcycle. I had always been very middle-class, and his kind just didn't seem my type. Anyway, he was nice to me, and I didn't think I deserved any better. He asked me to marry him. I did.

After three years of misery, I divorced him. I decided I didn't want anything from that marriage either. I just wanted out, fast. Now, I'm scared. I'm a two-time loser. I don't ever want to make that last mistake again. What do you think I should do?

In Sally's case, she forgot desperation and haste make waste. She rushed into things without the benefit of due deliberation. She immersed herself in any environment, provided there was some semblance of immediate comfort. She did not attempt to make decisions from an objective point of view. She gave into her most immediate emotions and sought a quick-fix to her sense of impending doom. Even now, she seems more interested in luxuriating in self-pity and asking others to look out for her than moving forward on her own. Although a victim of two divorces, there was no evidence Sally ever exercised self-control. She neither showed she had the spirit to fight nor an interest in getting an objective view of her life.

To have control over oneself (to act autonomously) is not a matter of doing what one wants. It is a matter of acting on the basis of compelling reason. There is nothing new about this idea, yet too many people fail to appreciate its meaning. Over two millennia ago, Aristotle pointed out we are constituted of both intellect and desires. In self-actualized human beings, reason reigns over the appetites. This does not mean people must become robot-like and deny their desires. It is a prescription for optimizing the fulfillment of desires. For example, a person may enjoy casual conversations with others. The person rightly believes a glass of wine helps people to relax while speaking freely and comfortably with others. The wine may stimulate many desires and tempt the person to seek more fulfillment. If reason is in control, the person concludes the experience of the moment may turn sour if he or she gives way to gross over-indulgence. If reason is abandoned, the pleasure-seeker suffers.

Sally gave total reign to her desires. She tried to accommodate whatever seemed comforting at the time. Until she learns to appreciate fully the importance of acting autonomously, it is unlikely she will take control of her life and fight back. Without the ability or will to fight back, she cannot plan a happy life.

Fighting the Right Fight

While the details of other stories may differ, the theme remains the same: until the divorcee effectively fights back, and against the right target, he or she has no hope for a satisfying life-plan. A friend confessed he was fortunate to realize the importance of fighting back early during the course of his divorce. Two weeks after his divorce began, this thirty-ish university researcher increased the number of miles he ran each week and began eating a Spartan-like diet of wholesome, nutritious foods. He initiated a program of weight training, stopped watching television, and began volunteering in a program for the terminally-ill at a local hospital. This last he said he did because dying was something he always feared:

> By confronting a fear and doing some good at the same time, I sensed I was forcing myself to fall under ever greater personal control. It was months later before I fully realized how much good I had done myself by doing these things. Not only did I begin feeling happier, I got healthier. Four months after the divorce, contrary to my doctor's advice, I had a complete physical, lab tests and all. The doctor marveled at the results. Every feature of my body was in perfect working order! My cholesterol was 162, triglycerides were 82, blood pressure, glucose tolerance, pulse, everything was remarkably in order. All this despite the fact that the doctor warned that my system would be "out of whack" and my lab tests abnormal because of the stress of divorce. "What is the secret?" he asked. "I don't know," I said. "Just being happy I guess."

After talking to so many others with this spirit, it becomes evident happiness is a function of assuming control over one's own destiny. Be reasonable, and you will be happier as a result. In divorce, it is reasonable to fight back. And it is reasonable to fight back *with honor*. The right fight is one meticulously planned, not one filled with rage, panic, fear, or other debilitating emotions.

Choosing a Mercenary

Before concluding this chapter, let me add one caveat. Be aware your lawyer does what *you* need to do. Divorce attorneys are hired guns. After all, who is going to hire a lawyer who is kindly disposed and, as a consequence, routinely loses his client's property and custody claims? The bottom line in the practice of family law is your attorney's ability to get what you want from your spouse while protecting your holdings. Divorce is adversarial for the clients and competitive for the lawyers. While the estranged couple may at times hate each other, this is seldom the case for the lawyers, and thank goodness since divorces benefit from calm, cool-headed thinking. While the disputants may be too emotional, the lawyers are generally unemotional and thoughtful. It becomes a problem for the client if the competitiveness of a lawyer becomes excessive.

One forty-year-old civil servant, Herb, said when he was seeking counsel, he came across a lawyer who wanted to hire a detective to spy on his wife and take pictures—that very weekend. The reason for the rush was Herb's wife was in charge of a medical conference that weekend. As such, she would be expected to socialize with the conference participants in the evening. This would involve having a drink in the hotel lounge and maybe dancing once or twice during the evening. It would not involve sexual encounters, flirtations or even cheek-to-cheek dancing. Herb balked at the suggestion. He explained there would be nothing for the detective to see. The lawyer insisted. He explained a woman having drinks in a hotel lounge and dancing would not look like a good mother to a judge. Herb objected. He said he and his wife had never been unfaithful to one another. He resented the fact such pictures would portray her as something she was not. The lawyer again insisted, saying since this case was likely to involve a custody battle, the man should use whatever resources were at his disposal. Herb admits he hesitated for a minute. He did want custody of the children. His wife was cruelly divorcing him simply because "she wanted her life back." Why, he thought, did she deserve their children and the benefit of his sense of decency? Finally, Herb decided he could not live with himself if he won "at all costs." Some costs are just too high.

Herb's decision was the first step towards fighting the right fight. He would be the loser if he deprived his wife of a fair fight for their children. He would know he and his lawyer acted unscrupulously and showed themselves to be willing to do anything for their own ends. Herb could not help but wonder what sort of parent he would make if that was how he gained custody. Herb responsibly sought another attorney more attuned to his principles.

I have learned of two other cases in which attorneys insisted their clients hire detectives to collect compromising photographs. In each case, the clients were told, respectively, "A single photograph is worth a thousand words" and "There is always a worthwhile photograph a good detective can take." In neither of these cases was there any reason to suspect the spouse of wrongdoing. Lawyers sometimes forget divorcees have more at stake than courtroom victory.

The reader should not conclude divorce attorneys are, by profession, a crafty and unscrupulous lot. There are a few such individuals, but you don't have to hire them. You hire a lawyer to represent and counsel you. Even the most well-meaning lawyer may initiate strategies you later detest. Don't let that happen. Don't abdicate responsible vigilance in the management of your own case. You need to form the policy under which you expect your lawyer to work. If that policy is unsatisfactory to either you or your lawyer, you need to find a more compliant counselor or reassess the wisdom of your policy.

When the subject of legal strategy or the details of a motion exceed your understanding, it is best to leave such matters in the hands of your lawyer. Once you and your former spouse agree in principle, leave the remaining technical considerations in the hands of your lawyers. When considering general policy, it is your responsibility to formulate the appropriate agenda since it is your life and integrity which are at issue.

Conclusion

Your first step in recovering from divorce will be determined by when and how you fight back. Recovering from divorce is not like recovering from disease. People often recover from disease with no residual effect, but the same cannot be said for divorce.

Divorce scars, and it can scar permanently. In this respect, recovering from divorce is analogous to recovering from an operation. Every operation leaves behind scar tissue. Following a successful operation, the scar tissue remaining has minimal effect on the quality of life subsequently enjoyed by the patient. In unsuccessful operations, the patient's quality of life is severely limited by the residual scar tissue. So it is even in a successful divorce: the psyche of the divorcee will be undeniably scarred. Happily, the scar will not destroy the divorcee's prospects for future contentment. On the other hand, in a divorce gone badly, the divorcee finds the scars reflect a greatly diminished capacity for happiness. As a deterrent against the deforming potential of divorce, fight back. However, when fighting back, identify the right target and proceed with the right intent.

The real target in the fight is yourself. Fight with honor. When the divorce is over, you will be by yourself. It would be a shame if your actions during the fight leave you a despicable loser. Prepare for the fight as you would for any athletic competition: eat well, exercise, place yourself under a strict regimen of self-discipline and control. Practice thinking positive thoughts about yourself. Specifically, practice seeing yourself as both a happy and an honorable person. Begin thinking about how you want to live as a single person.

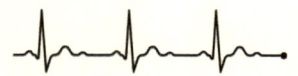

4

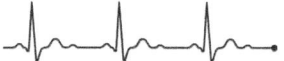

The Furies — Meeting Your Enemies

The emotions following upon the heels of divorce have been studied extensively by psychologists, sociologists and psychiatrists. Much is known about them and so little reason to rehash that material here. This book is for the lay person working his or her way through divorce. The purpose in discussing the post-divorce emotions is only to alert the reader to their occurrence; it is not to study them at length in the sterile and antiseptic manner of a scientist. This chapter describes how the negative effects of the furies can be avoided.

In a play entitled *The Flies*, Jean Paul Sartre describes the existential hero walking off toward the horizon knowing he will be plagued by flies biting and gnawing at his flesh forever. For reasons unknown to any but true believers in existentialism, the hero voluntarily undertakes this action. Presumably, he does so because the decision is contrary to all social influences and reason and, therefore, solely a function of the hero's will. The point for our purposes is once the hero's decision is made, there is no turning back. This is often the case with divorce.

The person who initiates a divorce may believe he/she has brought a tragic era in life to an end. It is an end. But what follows is often the commencement of an equally tragic era akin to a gnawing of one's psychological flesh. Divorce also thrusts the person being rejected into a tragic era and he/she must recover from betrayal and suffer the onslaught of other post-divorce emotions.

In Greek mythology, a trio of petty, vicious women have considerable power and ability to confuse and frustrate anyone coming into their presence. These women are known as the Furies. It seems the emotions which plague divorcing people are much like the Furies. Their role in people's lives is inevitable, and their attacks are ruthless and unpredictable. However, unlike the Furies of mythology, the furies of divorce are more numerous and… they are real, far too real.

The furies of divorce are guilt, grief, hate, anger, jealousy, and fear. There are lesser furies which badger some, but these are the principal ones plaguing the divorcee. In mythology, the Furies are each different and each has her own peculiar way of addressing the victim. There is no set order in which the Furies present themselves. The furies of divorce are similarly idiosyncratic. Some studies have tried to construct a post-divorce stage theory in which the antagonistic emotions of divorce appear one after another. However, most divorcees deny there is any pattern.

The announcement of divorce and the other party's response determines the nature of the furies' attack. The initial events of the divorce determine the intensity of the first encounter with a fury. Sooner or later, every divorcee will duel with each of the furies in turn. Sometimes the furies attack one at a time, sometimes in unison. When attacked by the furies, a person must resist losing control. Drink and drugs may, for the moment, distract the divorcee from these attacks. All that is illusory; sooner or later, the divorcee must address the furies.

Belief in the characters of mythology served to direct the actions of people in ancient Greece just as belief in the reality and intensity of grief determines, in part, the actions of today's divorcee. Because the furies of divorce are not substantive, it is difficult to know exactly how to respond. The action of the furies seems to originate outside the person, yet the meaning of what happens is personally contrived. While outside events may pique our interest and set the emotions racing, once provoked, the furies work their own mischief. The more havoc the fury wreaks, the more lengthy and difficult the post-divorce recovery. It is important to anticipate the furies' appearance and plan an appropriate and immediate defense to their vengeful attacks.

Although there is some excellent scientific literature on the characteristic features of the furies, people should consider simple examples which illuminate the distinctive features of each fury because it is essential to the recovering divorcee. You cannot respond to a destructive emotion until you have a more palpable sense of what you are up against.

Before discussing the furies, a more general word on emotions is in order. An emotion is an active "feeling of the mind" accompanied by physiological changes in the body. This feeling of the mind occurs after making a judgment about some state of affairs. For example, if you see a married man make a pass at a young, innocent-looking waitress, you may get angry or at least indignant. As you watch the philanderer's actions you *conclude* he has engaged in a deliberate misdeed. Your conclusion causes your heart rate to increase, your face to flush and other electric skin responses to occur as well. Your judgment and feeling response are connected. In contrast, attitudes and moods may possess some but not all of these characteristics. For example, your attitude toward people who cheat on their spouses may be held dispassionately. You may speak of it at length and even analyze it, but it need not produce any accompanying feelings. Given appropriate stimulus from the outside world, an attitude may predispose someone to experience a certain emotion. By themselves, however, attitudes may be held coolly while emotions never are. When you possess an attitude, you may have no particular person or event in mind. You are simply admitting to having a predisposition to judge an individual person or act in a certain way.

Moods possess some of the qualities of both emotions and attitudes, but not all. For example, after watching a philanderer work his mischief, you may not only become angry but you may find throughout the day your experience is contaminated by your earlier anger. You are in an angry mood.

When in an angry mood, it is not just further acts of philandering that excite you to harsh judgment, but rather your whole manner of responding to a wide range of stimuli reflects vague feelings associated with your earlier anger. For example, later in the day your spouse may say you are having leftovers for dinner. You may suddenly display unexpected anger. "I'm tired of leftovers! I want real food!" You and your spouse are both startled by your outburst. You then find yourself apologizing for being such a beast. "I'm sorry. I don't know what got into me." You plead, "I guess I've just been in a bad mood all day."

A mood preserves the residual effects of an emotion. For example, subdued but less well-defined physiological changes (such as blood pressure elevation and depressed immune responsiveness) may persist as long as one is "in a mood." In addition, one's "feeling of mind" is in an agitated state. Finally, moods are somewhat like attitudes because they do predispose one to making certain kinds of judgments although to a wide range of causes rather than those associated with specific attitudes. Many things can provoke new outbursts of anger, not just other episodes of philandering. A negative attitude toward cheating, in contrast, is only activated in consideration of a specific cause. Notice that people may excuse another's indiscriminately bad behavior by saying, "Oh, he's just in a bad mood. He's angry at the world." To describe another's attitude, speakers generally identify the immediate cause, a predisposition to make specific kinds of judgment under rather limiting circumstances; for example, we might say, "He has a negative attitude toward cheating." In other words, an attitude predetermines the nature of your reactions to a specific set of events whereas a mood affects your orientation to much of the world in general.

Health and well-being are more affected by emotions and moods than by attitudes in most cases. Emotions are *intense* and immediate. If my lover has just agreed to marry me, I may feel "filled with delight." I know I am happy, and the endorphins surging through my brain make my body a pleasant repository for the happy feelings of my mind. Much later, I may find I remain in a happy mood for quite some time even though the previous production of endorphins has dramatically decreased, and my lover's approval long receded from my immediate memory. In addition, my heart rate may increase when I am caught up in the midst of my happy emotion and decrease comfortably below normal much later when I'm still in a happy mood. Nevertheless, the persistence of the happy mood suggests the endorphins or some other neurochemical stimulant continue to provide me with comfort of mind.

Similarly, if my lover "breaks up" with me, I may feel overwrought (the emotion of grief). My respiration, blood pressure, perspiration, and heart rate may increase dramatically. Weeks later, I may feel sad (the mood of grief). My emotional, physiological and mental states may all show signs of diminished capacity for calm and rational thought and an increased capacity for illness and anxiety. The object of my grief may elude me from time to time, but some persistent physical discomfort and psychological anxiety remain.

Emotions may bring about heart attacks while moods insidiously nurture or aggravate a person's propensity for heart disease. Both emotions and moods must be carefully managed. The management of emotions and moods depend ultimately on the attitudes people form. Attitudes serve as the bedrock for, and are the precursors of, both emotions and moods.

Attitudes structure the tendency to evaluate experience in one way rather than another. Accompanying nearly every evaluation is an attendant emotion. Every emotion has the potential to provoke a mood. To put your moods and emotions under control, begin by reviewing the attitudes you possess. If you are harboring a self-destructive attitude, identify it and then change it.

Very quickly during divorce, one must learn to respond to the sharpness of destructive emotions. These destructive emotions are the furies. The emotions destroy the divorcee's outlook on life and, momentarily at least, drive him or her out of control. To the extent divorcees control the furies (and not simply suppress them), they lessen the severity of the following destructive moods. As divorcees learn new guidelines for appraising events affecting them (new attitudes), they will be victimized less often by the furies and subsequent lingering moods.

How the announcement of a divorce is made determines largely the quality of life divorcees experience throughout the first few days of separation. Psychologists say nearly all divorcees experience what I have dubbed the "Furies of Divorce." These are the divorce-related emotions of hate, anger, fear, guilt, and grief. The divorcee does not immediately experience all of these at once. But sooner or later, the furies will stealthily hunt down the divorcee. They will attack both individually and as a marauding, chaotic horde, nipping and biting at the divorcee's psyche until there is nothing left.

The first fury to launch an attack is a function of the "official" announcement of divorce. The perpetrator of the divorce may confront anger first. In contrast, the object of the divorce action usually confronts guilt first. Within as little as twenty-four hours following the announcement, each may experience the other fury. For example, as one twenty-six-year old woman with raven hair, blue eyes and a propensity for honest and direct communication told me:

> I had just fixed dinner. It was his favorite. He was just weeks away from graduating from medical school. It was a very happy time for us. When he finished eating, he told me he had found another woman, a nurse at his hospital. He said he was sorry but that he was going to divorce me and marry her. He said he knew how much I put up with in helping him get through medical school. He also said he knew I would understand. Then he said, 'Do you think we should sleep in separate beds until I move out?' I screamed at him to get out now! I never wanted to see him again! That night, I stomped around the house hating him and every minute I had ever spent with him. The next day, I worried that my over-reaction may have sent him into the arms of his lover, depriving me of my marriage forever. And I felt guilty that I acted hatefully towards him.

In this case, hate arrived first. Then the young woman was beset by guilt. She said she later grew angry again because she allowed herself to feel guilt and depression dwelling on the idea her life had fallen into shambles. Each fury competed for her attention. While under the influence of each new fury, she rationalized a previous attack from the perspective of the most recent marauder, hate from guilt, fear from hate, grief from guilt, and so on in what seemed to be an endless cycle. This experience is not at all unique nor limited to a specific social class.

A tiny thirty-three-year old woman named Beverly had just begun a successful career in the corporate world. Her husband had already proved himself a competent entrepreneur. He worked long and hard each day. At night and even on weekends, he was often too tired to spend much time with her. Still, he provided them both with a lavish lifestyle. He was four years older than his wife. They had met in high school where Burt was an athlete and Beverly a cheerleader. As the years wore on, Beverly came to believe she had become more of a person. She also believed Burt had lost sight of everything important outside of work. She dismissed him now as a mere automaton. Divorce seemed the only way for each to fulfill his or her own destiny. When Beverly told Burt she wanted a divorce, she explained there was no other man. She also reassured him there was no failure on his part and no reason for him to feel guilty. She told him he was a good man, but they had just taken different paths in life. Now, she declared, it was their time to part ways.

Shocked and dismayed, Burt pleaded with her to stay. He became self-deprecating and immersed himself in expressions of guilt and anxiety. Predictably, the next day, when his guilt had ebbed somewhat, he became furious. In a short time, the rest of the furies raised their ugly heads, and he wallowed in confusion, grappling with each in turn, only to be attacked again and again by the others.

Beverly said she feared Burt might hurt himself but insisted her fear was not a form of guilt. On numerous occasions, she repeated she was doing the right thing. Nevertheless, she admitted worrying she had been indelicate in her handling of Burt. Beverly also admitted in bed that night, she lay awake fearing she had made a terrible mistake. Although she was not sure what the mistake might be, somehow it seemed she must be guilty of one. Despite her disclaimers to the contrary, it was evident Beverly was wrestling with feelings of guilt every bit as much as fear. Regardless of the situation, no one is excused entirely from some confrontation with each of the furies.

In situation after situation, it did not make any difference what role one played in the announcement of the divorce. Both the initiator and respondent experienced the wrath of the furies. Once a divorce begins, one of the furies will attack and determine the emotional atmosphere of the next few hours and even days. There is no way to circumvent this torment and, usually, no way to fight one's way back to a blissful marriage. Once a spouse commits to divorce as he or she once did to marriage, a separation will occur. The furies begin their work with the announcement of the divorce. However, it is not until the next few days have passed that their full collective force becomes known to both parties. When this occurs, a happy reconciliation is all but impossible. Life with the furies begins. Take this opportunity to think about each one at length. The reader of this book has probably already met each fury informally.

Guilt

Consider the emotion of guilt, which is the first fury experienced by many divorcees. Guilt is the feeling attendant upon wrong-doing. Though our attitudes toward divorce have become more tolerant over the years, no one is yet likely to argue divorce is a good thing. Some divorces may be unavoidable and so tolerance is in order. Nevertheless, marriages are supposed to be good things, and their failure a bad thing.

Humans are, by nature, rational to varying degrees. Part of what it means to be rational is to be ready to evaluate the merit of people, deeds, and events. If divorce is a bad thing, then presumably people who divorce are doing a bad thing. They are guilty of wrongdoing. There are two relevant attitudes at work here. The common attitude is divorce is a bad thing. An enlightened attitude of tolerance demands only those people guilty of causing a divorce merit condemnation for their actions. Since nearly every person in contemporary America shares these attitudes, most divorcees believe it is important not to be identified (in their own minds or in the minds of others) as THE CAUSE of a divorce. Most divorcees go to great lengths to assign guilt for the divorce to their spouse or a third party (kids, lovers, in-laws, etc.) or, at the very least, they do all they can to avoid assuming as much blame as possible.

A year after her divorce, Sherri, a twenty-eight-year old oil and gas account executive explained:

> Six weeks after we were married, my husband wanted to make love to me while he wore my bra and panties. He was serious! I couldn't stay married to a nut like that. We had dated for six months be-

fore we got married, and he never did anything like that. I didn't want to divorce him, but, golly, you can't let yourself get trapped in a situation like that. What else could I expect if I didn't leave then?

The reader may dismiss this case as being uncharacteristic both because of the bizarre behavior of the husband and the brief duration of the marriage. Nevertheless, what is important is the fact Sherri felt compelled to give an explanation and assign blame for the divorce even though she was talking to someone who was very nearly a total stranger to her. Guilt rests on the doorstep of every divorce, and every divorcee fears it may find permanent lodging within the soul.

Three years after his divorce, a thirty-six-year old lawyer, Frank, confessed:

> The divorce was all my fault. Dorothy was the perfect wife. She was always faithful to me and great with the kids. She was so good with the kids I didn't have the heart to fight for them when we got divorced. I just can't say enough good things about her. She's a good-looking woman—for her age. I really had no reason to divorce my wife, I was just a louse...
>
> Well, I really wasn't a "louse." I mean, I was a good father, and I did take care of her well. I was usually faithful, except for a couple of business trips, but, my God, after eleven years of marriage, everyone's likely to mess around if they have the chance, right? Anyway, I had this girl working in the office as a sort of "Jack of all trades." She was very bright, beautiful and was going to start law school in the

fall. She was learning so much about the law so quickly. Dorothy would never try to learn anything about it. You know, she'd just do one of those dumb giggles whenever legal issues came up and say she didn't understand any of it. She just never tried! She just wanted to be a small-scale socialite and ace-number one Mom.

Anyway, I never set out to chase Gloria. We just worked very closely together. Finally, one night after work we were having a drink, and we just knew we were in love. I really didn't want to hurt Dorothy, but what choice did I have? I couldn't stay with someone I didn't love. Anyway, these things just happen. No one's really at fault.

This case illustrates the fear each divorcee has of inheriting a lifetime of guilt. Recall the lawyer freely admitted his guilt: "I was a louse." On the other hand, he went on to excuse his culpability first by portraying his office romance as an innocent accident. If that wasn't hypocritical enough, he went on to say what he did is what anyone would do in such circumstances. (I wonder what he advises his children about doing what everyone else allegedly does?)

The point in such gerrymandering is to avoid assuming the burden of guilt permanently. Intellectually, Frank recognized he failed to protect the life-project he and Dorothy set out to achieve. He also realized, perhaps subconsciously, he could not handle shouldering all the blame for the divorce. Consequently, he ends his account by shifting some guilt to Dorothy and dismissing the rest. If one were to speak with Dorothy, one could expect her to accept some of the blame. When being divorced by one's "life partner," even in a case as clear-cut as this, most people wonder, "What did I do? What else could I have done to hold things together?" Hence, while Frank tries to elude blame, Dorothy will seek to share in it.

All divorcees experience guilt. But surely some are not deserving of it. What should the innocent and victimized do? Just set it aside? They cannot any more than you, the reader, can succeed in obeying the following instructions. For the next three minutes, place this book aside and concentrate on the command:

> "Do not think about monkeys!
> Do not think about monkeys.
> Do NOT think about monkeys.
> Particularly, do NOT think about monkeys
> playing around a barrel."

Continue repeating these words to yourself. What happens? You begin thinking about the very thing you were instructed not to think about. The same is true with assigning guilt in a divorce. You cannot free yourself of guilt until you finish assigning blame. After all, it seems only reasonable if a person has been at fault, in any way, then he or she is blameworthy. Seemingly, most people cannot rest until they know what proportion of the guilt is their respective share. This is not a psychologically sound decision, but for most people it is compelling—-at least for a while.

What are the options? Should one roll over and give guilt free reign over one's life? No. Instead, the divorcee should recognize the emotion of guilt for what it is, a fury. Guilt is a fury attacking divorcees who should prepare an appropriate counterattack.

After you have come to the realization the divorce is inevitable, take a day and fully confront all possible assignments of guilt. Do not try to determine the possible "right" distribution of guilt. That distribution is too difficult to determine even for an objective observer and that you are not. In trying to get the right distribution, you may be too cowardly or you may be too vindictive when assessing. In either case, you will do little more than increase your own anguish. Instead, begin by assigning all blame for the divorce to yourself. Do not let up. Be as exhaustive as possible of all your faults. Believe for a few hours that *"You, and you alone, are the sole cause of your divorce!"* When you have exhausted any further cause for blame, it is time to remove the hair shirt. Your penance is complete. Turn now to considering your mate.

When you think about it, *really think about it,* you know, *"The divorce is entirely the fault of my spouse!* I may have had some slight foibles but not enough to cause the divorce. He/she is the cause of this divorce." When you have exhausted all recollection of the relevant misdeeds of your spouse, it is time to remove your executioner's hood.

You can expect to be thoroughly fatigued from this day long inquisition, but only at this point will you be prepared to ask yourself the most profound and important question of all: *"What does it all matter?"* Who cares who was at fault? The fact is you are getting (have gotten) divorced. Are you doing anything today you should feel guilty about? If so, stop; if not, then there is no need to assign blame. If your spouse is currently doing something blameworthy, it is no longer a concern of yours unless it is directed towards you, in which case you must protect yourself and your family usually through some sort of legal channel.

Are you planning to do anything you should feel guilty about? Again, if so, stop. If not, set yourself to making today and tomorrow days you *will be proud of*. Since you can never really *know* what planning is taking place in the mind of your spouse, it is a waste of your valuable time to try to ferret out his or her intentions or plans for you much less evaluate the moral merit of such. The more quickly you realize building the next part of your life requires all your attention and that the past is now a mere distraction, the sooner you will begin creating a solid and pleasant life style.

The divorce and its causes recede further into history with each new day. Reviewing the past for the purpose of assigning guilt will do nothing to build a better today or a better tomorrow. Once you follow the exercise recommended above, there will no longer be any reason to torture yourself with questions of assigning just desserts. You will have paid your debt, if any is owed and, vicariously, you will have exacted from your spouse all the grounds you could ever want for his or her condemnation. Most importantly, you will have concluded the issue of moral evaluation for offenses long past no longer merits your continued attention.

Hate and Anger

Often when we play the game of assigning guilt in matters of divorce, we realize the emotions of hate and anger are lurking about everywhere. While the two emotions are in fact quite different, people habitually refer to the two as identical experiences. Sometimes they describe hate as an intense form of anger. This confusion distracts the subject's attention from the actual nature of each and makes mustering an appropriate response more difficult.

If I conclude I am responsible for all or part of the divorce, I may be *angry* with myself. In the wake of divorce, I may *hate* the fact I ever married. Anger involves moral indignation and an expectation things can be done to compensate the aggrieved. Hate involves a desire to obliterate from the speaker's experience some person, place, policy, relationship, institution, or action. Properly speaking, you may hate many things, but anger can only be directed at persons or communities of persons. Neither necessarily turns into the other because of the passage of time or intensity.

For example, hate is not a matter of harboring intense anger for a long period of time. I may honestly say I hate commercial television. In speaking so, I exhibit no intense feeling whatsoever. I am doing nothing more than announcing my desire that commercial television should end. Similarly, I may coolly hate my spouse even though all feelings of anger have long since abated. In contrast, I may be angry with my spouse but not feel at all hateful. Often a person feels both, but this is not necessarily so. I may be *angry* my spouse ran off with another, but that need not lead to hate. If she were to return and make amends, my anger might diminish. Anger often leads to hate, but hate rarely leads to anger. The two emotions are often associated, but they are not exclusively so. They are not identical nor is one a name for an intense version of the other.

A thirty-one-year old laboratory director, Janet, relates the following account of anger:

> I became discouraged with my husband. He seemed to have no ambition whatsoever. He was

good at what he did, and I tried to get him to advance into administration. He said he liked what he did and was going to stay where he was.

His job took him away from me for long periods of time. I wanted him with me. I believe he was always faithful to me, but it just didn't seem to matter to him if we were together or not. After many months of insisting that he do something different with his life, I told him I wanted a divorce. He said he didn't want a divorce, but if that was what I wanted, he wouldn't stand in my way. He made me furious. Why didn't he fight for me?

I started the divorce. He went along with it to the point of giving me everything I asked for—some of which even I thought was unreasonable! His continued cooperation just made me angrier and angrier. When I look back on it, I know that if he had confronted me, told me he loved me and wouldn't give me up, I would still be married. Instead, all he did was cooperate and go in his room to drink. After the divorce, I felt guilty for having caused it. However, every time I felt guilty, I'd get angry. "Why didn't he fight for me?" It's funny. I never hated him. Even now I think I could still love him, but if I think of him for even a minute or two, I start getting angry. Sometimes I get so angry I end up hating myself for divorcing him and also for marrying him in the first place. I just don't understand someone like that. I guess the divorce was the best thing.

In contrast to this experience of anger (and the following self-hate), compare the following account of hate. Shelly was a thirty-nine-year old hospital administrator. She had been divorced for over a year when she offered the following account:

> I divorced him because he was a jerk. We rushed into marriage when we were barely out of college. We were just too young. If I wasn't pregnant when we married, I would never have gone through with it. He's a jerk. I wish he were dead. That's how I think of him… as dead. I hate him, and I hate everything I associate with him. It's just like he made a big hole in my life.

In this case, Shelly's emotions are no more intense than those of Janet. However, whereas Janet was offended by her ex's behavior she remained open to some sort of redress of grievances. This suggests anger is Janet's emotional tormentor, whereas Shelly wants to forget her ex entirely. Shelly is not angry, she hates.

Both hate and anger are potentially intense emotions which consume considerable psychological and physical energy. As long as one is subject to fits of either, the prospects for recovery are limited. Recurring fits of hate and anger are destructive to future self-development. If the divorcee is overcome by either hate or anger, he or she is losing the present and risking the future for an unchangeable past. To hedge against such loss in the face of hate and/or anger, the best thing to do is either undertake an intellectually challenging task or engage in a strenuous physical activity.

A person cannot command an emotion to stop any more than he or she can stop thinking about monkeys upon command.

You cannot obliterate the past on an instant's notice. Your past will continue to play a limited role in your future, and you should bear this in mind. If the divorce is final, any redress of grievances will be inconsequential. So what's the point of persistent anger? If the divorce is not final, don't let the reckless energy of anger cause you to fight dishonorably. If you do, your bouts of anger will probably lead to guilt. To become absorbed by hate will do nothing more than assure what you hate will remain before your mind's eye. If you truly want to remove an object from your world view, concentrate on those aspects of your world view you want to develop, not those you wish to delete. In the short run, escape from hate and anger is best achieved through distraction. Focus your body and mind on a consuming activity, leaving no room for these furies. In the long run, begin each day by thinking your way through to a change of attitude.

Fear

When hate, anger, and guilt are wreaking havoc in the divorcee's world, it is natural to *fear* you will lose control. Fear is the nastiest of the furies and meriting the most extensive discussion. Like guilt, fear seems to work in tandem with each of the other furies. People fear their feelings of hate or anger will destroy them. They fear they will never escape the guilt or jealousy caused by divorce. People fear their grief will lead to absolute despair. Divorcees fear they will never again be whole or share life with another. They fear getting sick and dying alone. Some fear their inability to manage personal business affairs. Others fear they have lost their looks, their vitality, or both. And, consequently, they fear they will never succeed as a single. Finally, in the worst cases, they begin fearing fear itself. Most disastrously, they may experience episodes of acute, undirected fear. This is known in psychiatric circles as generalized panic syndrome (GPS).

Agoraphobia (the earlier, misleading term for generalized panic syndrome) originally meant an irrational fear or phobia of the marketplace. Many see the single life as a place where people's personhood is bought and sold, approved or rejected. Many divorcees fear being single because they cannot imagine being on the market again. This fear can be avoided if they let go of the marketplace metaphor. With images in mind and attitudes in place, it is no wonder these people fear single life. This manifestation of fear can be avoided by shifting one's attitude away from single life as a place where deals are made. Instead, one can just as easily see single life as an opportunity for exploring a broad range of acquaintances and developing friendships. The attitudes divorcees nurture make them prone to be vulnerable to emotions both good and bad.

Agoraphobia (GPS) is not an exclusive by-product of commercial exchange. Nor is it a by-product of the personal experiences of crowds, expansive spaces, or strange and alienating environments. Some people experience panic attacks on their own doorstep or at the house and in the company of a close friend. Panic attacks seem to occur at any place or at any time the phobic feels insecure.

During an episode of GPS, the subject feels out of control. The person believes he or she is having a heart attack or is going to faint or become psychotic. It should be of some comfort to the phobic to know the technical literature reveals not a single instance of a person dying, going insane, or losing consciousness from a GPS episode.

Some researchers believe victims of GPS feel little control over large areas of their lives. Consequently, sufferers of GPS may unintentionally bring on their attacks by dwelling on the idea that they lack control. Bio-psychologists, cardiologists, and family doctors have become increasingly persuaded a patient's thinking has both an immediate and an accumulated effect on body chemistry and physical well-being. It is no longer hard to imagine then that *beliefs* about lack of control can lead to the physiological *sensation* of losing control.

Divorce may bring about the belief that one is losing control. As that belief becomes well-entrenched in the mindset of the divorcee, he or she evolves an attitude of diminished capacity. This attitude, in turn, may start the physiological sensation of losing control, of a mind about to go haywire, or a body about to fail. The relationships between divorce and episodes of acute fear or panic no longer seem so remote. Divorce may be a contributing factor in GPS. This is a matter currently attracting further research by social and medical scientists.

Bunny, a thirty-two-year old school teacher, who has been divorced for nearly three years, relates the following story:

> My husband and I never got along. We loved each other, but he was undependable. We had been married nine years. Throughout, he kept changing jobs. Sometimes he was promoted and sometimes he was fired. One year he might make over one hundred thousand dollars and the next year he might make eighteen thousand. He was always on the prowl, looking for that next big sale. I wanted him to get a job that was more stable, one that paid a salary and kept him at home. One day he blew up. He said he wanted a divorce. He said I should go my way and he should go his. We separated

for almost a year; then we got lawyers to make the divorce final. During that time neither he nor I dated anyone. He sent money home, but whenever we talked he was firm about never wanting to see me again.

One day, about a week before the divorce was finalized, I was in my car and stopped at a railroad crossing. Suddenly, I felt trapped. I never had this happen before. There was the train in front of me and cars to my left and in the rear. I started to get out of the car. I had to get away. I didn't know where I was going, I just had to get away. My heart was racing, my head was pounding. I thought I was getting dizzy. I sat back down in my car. I was confused. The train passed, and people started honking at me. One man came up and asked me if I needed help. I said I didn't know. Somehow, the police got there. I started feeling okay by then, but they insisted on following me home. They smelled my breath and asked me if I was taking any medicines.

I get these attacks about once a month now. My doctor says it's just worry, and he's given me some medicine, but I don't like to take it. Usually, the attacks come at night when I'm alone. I find it helps if I go into my daughter's room and sit on the floor next to her bed when they happen. When the attack subsides, I usually cry because I feel so stupid. I also worry that I may really be getting sick or be losing my mind. Then I wouldn't be able to take care of my daughter. It's all so scary I don't even like to think about it. I also worry that if my husband finds out, he'll use the information to get my daughter from me.

Bunny appears normal. Even while relating this story, she seemed to be a model of good judgment and confident self-control. She recently won a teaching award at her school and was promoted to department chair. To her peers and the rest of the world, she is a dependable and competent individual. From her perspective, she is losing control.

I do not believe it is mere coincidence Bunny's GPS began with her impending divorce. Her fears of losing control over her marriage and life seem to be intimately tied in with her GPS experiences. The prisons imposed on sufferers of GPS, such as Bunny, are of their own making. This is not to suggest GPS victims are guilty of some evil. Rather, the attitudes they've developed leave them victim to these emotional difficulties. Freedom from GPS can be purchased by confronting one's fears and fighting back.

Bunny did not fight back. She did not try to change her attitudes. She was imprisoned by her fears and things got worse. Her self-imposed cell shrank. Researchers of GPS note this is common. Untreated GPS is unstable. It leads to greater frequency and intensity of attack and a shrinking of the victim's "zone of comfort."

Bunny did not fight back during her divorce. She felt herself more and more under the control of outside influences, and soon she was caught in the grip of acute episodes of fear. Since she didn't fight back, she is now to the point where she fears each new attack of fear itself. Divorce changed Bunny's view of herself. These new beliefs turned up in attitudes that made Bunny vulnerable to the most devastating of all the furies, fear. Her world has turned ugly.

Experts in the study of GPS believe as many as twenty percent of the adult American population experience an attack of GPS sometime during their lives. Since far fewer than twenty percent of the population suffer from chronic GPS, there must be some way of avoiding the tyranny of fear, a way Bunny has yet to discover.

In contrast to Bunny's story, consider the following story told by Kim, a thirty-nine-year old night-school teacher. Kim is a man who was hell-bent on becoming frail and sickly at an early age and facing a premature death.

> I had been going through divorce for about six weeks. I felt very blue from time to time thinking about how much I was going to miss my wife and kids. I didn't like being around people anymore. I saw all the people I wanted to in class. I did not want any well-meaning do-gooders prying into my life. I wanted to be alone with my own melancholy. One day, after a committee meeting at work, I was driving home. I had two hours before my next class, and I wanted to be alone. Traffic was heavy. I was brooding about being kicked out of my own family. Suddenly, I felt trapped. My heart was racing. I broke out into a cold sweat. I genuinely believed I was having a heart attack! I couldn't figure out what to do.
>
> Since I live next to a hospital, I thought I should go home. If I were having a heart attack and needed to get to the hospital, I'd still be heading in the right direction. When I got home, I walked in and lay down on the floor. My pulse was up over 140 beats per minute. A half hour later it was 120 beats per minute and threatening to increase momentarily. I thought, "What should I do… go

to the hospital… call in sick and cancel class, then stay home and take care of myself… or should I go to work and risk dying?" I then began assessing the facts. I was a runner, a non-smoker, and a teetotaler. Neither of my parents had heart problems. I shouldn't be having one either.

I began thinking about agoraphobia. I knew agoraphobia is often mistaken for a heart attack. I knew I had been under a lot of stress and that could provoke a panic attack. I also knew that stress could provoke a heart attack. If it was a panic attack and I gave into it, I would probably be subject to more panic attacks in the future. On the other hand, if I confronted this one, then perhaps I could keep my life under control. I thought "If this is a heart attack and I try to go to work, I may die. Damn it," I announced to myself, "if it's a panic attack and I give into it, I'm liable to become an emotional cripple. If it's a heart attack, no one really cares whether I live or die anyway, so what the hell. If I'm going to die, I'll go out in style giving the best damn lecture my students ever heard!" With that, I got up, heart pounding and set off for work. I got more relaxed with each step. When I got to work, my doubts returned. With each doubt, my pulse went back up. "It's too late to turn back now," I cried to myself. "I'm going through with this." I walked into the classroom and threw everything I had into the lecture. After twenty minutes, I was doing fine. Each word was perfectly selected to follow on the heels of its predecessor. I felt tremendous peace and satisfaction. It's been nearly two years since that night, and I've never had another episode of fear. After that night, I believed I could take anything life, or my own body, could dish out. I don't know, maybe I just had some bad oysters for lunch that day and it destabilized my brain chemistry.

If we assume with Kim that he experienced a panic attack that night, then his efforts were just what was needed to avoid chronic GPS. Indeed, behavioral therapy for sufferers of GPS or any phobic-related syndrome aims at getting the phobic to confront his or her fears. This teacher defiantly confronted his fear. After this episode of acute fear, he had confidence, fight and no more room for this particular fury. Moreover, he got healthier and more robust than he had been for at least the past decade.

Divorce-related fear is not always acute. Most commonly, it is experienced as "chronic-fear," fear that "all is lost, my life is broken and nothing is left except to await a liberating death." Of course, divorce does not end life, but a person's chronic fear of addressing life as a single may keep the divorcee from enjoying the exhilaration of a well-kept, serene, and orderly life.

No divorcee can avoid the ravages of fear entirely. Divorce casts all the furies into the divorcee's life. By identifying the fury of fear and confronting it directly, a person can diminish its effects in short order. Although this is easier said than done, it can be done! And until the divorcee conquers divorce-related fear, recurring victimization will remain the order of the day.

Jealousy

Jealousy is rarely as vicious as the other furies. Everyone becomes jealous at the thought of his or her life partner romancing another. For some, the thought can drive them crazy. For others, it may make them uncomfortable, but they eventually become accustomed to the inevitability of the fact that an ex dates and may one day re-marry.

Jealousy is likely to assume two forms. Each is experienced in a sustained and intense fashion and, at other times, in a mild and transitory fashion. The form of jealousy most common is also the one most primitive in human nature.

In his classic sociological treatise of the early 1970s, *The Territorial Imperative*, author Robert Ardrey speculated that the establishment and protection of territorial rights is a central motivating force for all animal life, humans included. In the context of divorce, people feel they own the rights to a human "territory," i.e. another person. Sometimes this righteous feeling is vividly portrayed. No longer committed to the well-being of one's spouse, this form of jealousy nevertheless provokes resentment and hostility to the divorcee who is first stunned when seeing their ex with another. If the jealousy you feel is a response to your notion that territorial rights are being invaded, disabuse yourself of the belief and you will be free of this form of jealousy. As Barbara, a forty-year-old mother of two explained:

> I wanted the divorce. There was just nothing in me for him. For years, there was almost no sexual activity between us and when there was, I felt repulsed and dishonest in my efforts to satisfy him. A year after we divorced, I saw Howard at a public

social gathering. He was still short and pudgy. He was with an equally unattractive woman. Surprisingly, I felt jealous. I didn't love this man. I don't know if I ever did. Yet there I stood looking over at the two of them and feeling oddly jealous. Of course, in a few minutes I got over all that. Eventually, I became happy that he found someone. I don't hate him or anything. How do you hate a sad sack? He just represents a dumb decision in my life and one I'm glad to leave behind.

In this case the woman had no lingering feelings of love for her ex. Still, as she said, she was surprised by the fact that seeing him in this way could provoke a fleeting moment of jealousy. (How nice it would be if every divorcee's experience of jealousy could be so easily disposed.)

This rather extreme example illustrates two things. First, an encounter with some form of jealousy seems inevitable. Second, this kind of jealousy is easily shed when one recognizes he/she is wrestling with an egocentric preoccupation with territory "rights" to a person. When this misconception of "rights" is appreciated, one will no longer suffer from the illusion of loss.

The second form of jealousy is quite different. In this case, the divorce represents the dissolution of the sort of bonding central to the most ideal marriages. In this bonding, each person freely accepts the goals and interests of the other as goals and interests for oneself. In this state of "erotic love" (wherein one's most appealing sexual partner is also one's best friend), two people become so intimately bound together they genuinely assume one common project in life, namely, the satisfaction of one another's goals, interests and needs. They learn to share one conjointly extended sense of personhood. They still are two people of course, but, in many ways, they choose freely to address the world as two instances of one person or to recall Aristotle, it's when two people become one soul. In this rare form of bonding, each person is genuinely elated by the partner's success, not because it reflects well on the spouse but because it is good for the partner. Similarly, erotic lovers experience anguish (not sympathy) in the face of the partner's defeats. This, too, occurs not because such things reflect badly upon oneself but because each experiences the world through the lover's being as well as through one's own. Erotic love is the kind of bonding poets have sung about in Persia, Israel, India, and various Western cultures. It is a form of bonding some jaded divorcees are loathe to admit exists because such bonding is, for them, an opiate of the gullible masses; it is not something knowledgeable and worldly people can accept.

In today's world, to be "informed" often amounts to no more than becoming immersed in "pop" culture. In the effort to be oh-so-sophisticated, a person may become cynical and balk at the idea relationships of erotic love exist. The experience of divorce alone makes some people so cynical that the possibility of erotic love is denounced as sheer fantasy, a sort of hoped-for pipe-dream naively pursued by over-stimulated teenagers.

The tenderness and bonding occurring in truly erotic love has been a focus of literature from vastly diverse and remote cultures since before the time of Christ. Thus, we find in Arabic, Indian, Oriental, Egyptian, and Greek literature accounts of impassioned love. The societies may encourage monogamy or polygamy, heterosexual or homosexual relationships, but each recognizes that an especially unique bonding can occur in a union between lovers. Erotic love, the relationship marriage was designed to protect from intrusion, is cross-culturally illustrative of the best humans can be together.

When erotic love is destroyed by divorce, jealousy takes a form quite distinct from the territorial imperative. In this case, one's sense of personhood and self-esteem are both ruptured by the tragedy of divorce. When the common life project is dissolved, the estrangement following devastates each individual's life plan as well. In such cases, neither can easily answer the question, "What am I about?" The very idea one's spouse could seek union with another brings on a destructive confusion within the divorcee. "It's you and me against the world, honey," becomes "It's you and *someone else* against the world." "What about us? We were as one. Now, I feel less than a person!" These reactions and these unions have become so common even trained psychotherapists mistake them as instances of codependency. They may well be, but they are not pathologic or in need of "treatment."

The episodes of jealousy following the dissolution of erotic love are enduring and threaten one's very self-perspective. Fear often accompanies jealousy when the divorcee contemplates the loss of shared perspective with a former spouse.

In nearly all cases of jealousy, the next emotion to follow is hate. In the first type of jealousy, the hate aims at the loss of property rights the divorcee felt she or he had over the other. In the second type of jealousy, the hate aims at the divorcee's suspected loss of self-identity. In instances of the first type of jealousy-related hate, the jealous divorcee usually figures out his or her experience of jealousy is misconceived. Since no one can have any property rights over another person in the first place, there is no loss, no new reality to be obliterated from before the mind's eye. When this realization occurs to the divorcee, all hateful agitation is shortly relieved.

In instances of the second type of jealousy-related hate, the aggrieved party cannot even imagine how thinking different thoughts can relieve his or her obsession. This is understandable since jealousy-related hate of the first type is usually a consequence of previous infatuation, a "friendly-type" of love that too often suffices as a reason people marry. Their sense of loss can be recovered by simply re-calling assumed property rights over another person or by "re-assigning" them to a new partner. In contrast to this, people truly bonded by erotic love experience a sense of *timelessness* about their feelings. For them, the onslaught of divorce is incomprehensible. The timelessness of their commitment is replaced by a timelessness of loss, of lack of purpose and identity. As Roger Scruton, a leading philosopher of love, explains in his book *Sexual Desire,* there is no erotic love if either person can postulate the length of time he or she will be in love or the length of time it will take them to fall out of love or recover from unrequited love. Timelessness is part and parcel of erotic love and of the feelings surrounding the loss of an erotic love. Most divorcees can take heart in the fact it is unlikely they are leaving behind an erotic love, even if at first it certainly feels that way.

    The inability to envision an end to love or "two persons, one soul" occurs because in erotic love a person thoroughly meshes his or her life plans in a common project undertaken with an intended other. When the bond of erotic love is unexpectedly broken, the lovers flounder about for an inordinate length of time as each awkwardly attempts to reconstruct a new sense of self, a sense of self independent of the other. Shattered erotic love leads divorcees to act more like widows and widowers than like other divorcees.

    In erotic love, one does not try to *possess* the other, but one does *identify* with the other much in the way one identifies with one's own self. Consequently, abandonment by one's lover is felt as an abandonment or destruction of one's very self-concept.

A final note on erotic love: as Scruton explains, no one experiences erotic love without having that love reciprocated. Hardened veterans of divorce know how often people try to fool themselves reciprocity is present or one partner truly loved while the other did not. Indeed, cynics admonish anyone foolish enough to believe such symmetry ever exists in the topsy-turvy world of human relationships. Nevertheless, the romantic literature from separate cultures and spread over the millennia is replete with references to the existence of this special bond. Most people today—even those whose hearts have been repeatedly battered by divorce—continue pursuing romantic encounters in the *hopes* of achieving that singularly unique experience… erotic love.

How could erotic love have such universal appeal if it or something like it, did not exist? How is it most people know of at least one elderly couple who made it and are the envy of all who know them? It is the cynic who must convince the rest of the world that the believer has been tricked by a grand deceiver, that erotic love does not exist. For all the rest, erotic love exists and its failure is uncontrovertibly tragic.

In the ballet *La Sylphide* ("The Sylph"), the dancers show how often people, in their hurry to engage in romance, become mismatched with one another. The current generation's perception of "relationships" seems to be one where people separate or divorce when they realize they are mismatched. Unfortunately, divorce is not this simple. While infatuation is fickle and transient, erotic love is not. People bounce back from the dissolution of nearly any kind of relationship except, sometimes, erotic love.

Erotic love rarely ends in divorce. When it does, it is because one or both the lovers was severely traumatized and is unable to push forward with a fruitfully evolving concept of self. Without a strong concept of self, a person cannot undertake a project in which two selves operate as one corporate entity. A lawyer shared with me the following example of divorcing erotic lovers:

> Kelly and Hal had been married for eight years. They had one five-year-old daughter. Hal was thirty-one, handsome, athletic and of modest intelligence. He came from a broken home where each of his estranged parents continued to try to give him away to the other parent. He grew up living in bungalows and going to school in blue-collar neighborhoods. Kelly was twenty-eight-years old, athletic and gorgeous. She came from a family that was wealthy and afforded her many cultural and educational opportunities. She was never a particularly good student, but she went to the best private schools her academic record would allow. All who knew Hal and Kelly admired the love they seemed to share.
>
> During the seventh year of marriage, their second child died of pneumonia at the age of six months. Neither parent was at fault for the child's illness or death. There was no reason to believe that either had been neglectful toward the deceased child. Nevertheless, neither Kelly nor Hal could get over the idea that a healthy child born into a proper middle-class family could get sick and die of pneumonia. Kelly and Hal told their respective lawyers that after the infant's death they could not "get it together." Their sex life ended. Within six months, they were not even sleeping in the same room. Each whined that they still loved the other... they just could not live together. It took two and a half

years for Kelly and Hal to plod through the divorce. During this time, they would attend special affairs together and often seemed on the verge of a reconciliation—including at least two occasions on which they began living together again. Rarely did either one date. Each seemed equally concerned with the well-being of the surviving child and each was supportive of the other's parenting style. Occasionally, legal proceedings would be delayed because one or the other would feign concern with the division of property. When the divorce was finalized, it seemed anti-climactic and indicative of no change in the couple's relationship. Both attorneys remained convinced that someday Kelly and Hal would reconcile.

So why the divorce? There was no apparent reason other than the inability of the parents to deal with the death of their child. When apart, Kelly and Hal longed for each other. Their frequent "outings" seemed filled with joy and happiness. Nevertheless, any attempt at living together reminded them of their shared but dreaded past. This marriage was broken by something neither spouse had any control over; certainly, there was no dissonance between the two personalities. Even their different backgrounds seemed to strengthen their union. Kelly admired Hal's commitment to the simple joys of family life. She admitted that previously she took many of these things for granted. Hal alerted her to the importance of family meals, Easter egg hunts, and all the things he could never count on when he was growing up. For his part, Hal never ceased praising Kelly for encouragement. She urged him to get his master's degree and to continue taking evening classes for general self-improvement. What this case shows is divorce is not always a consequence of wrongdoing or even mismatched personalities. It is sometimes nothing more than a chance mutation in human history.

People who once enjoyed the benefits of erotic love feel overwrought with intense jealousy. If one talks to enough divorcees, one learns this, as Hilda, a fifty-one-year old woman explained (two years after her divorce):

> Often I felt no hate, anger, or guilt. Sometimes I just felt paralyzed by the thought of him being with someone else. I just couldn't stop thinking that "I" and "we" all had the same meaning. How could "we" be out with another woman? I also used to worry about what I would do now. All "my" plans had always been "our" plans. I'll make it okay; it is tough though. What I do is pretend he's dead. I still love him, I guess I always will—even if I remarry. You just don't throw away twenty-three years of marriage. I know I'm still a part of his life and always will be. There just aren't enough years left to rid each other from our lives.

The jealousy Hilda expresses is not the territorial imperative. She is not incensed at being deprived of property rights. In addition, she never identified "her" plans exhaustively with "his" plans. She very clearly saw her identity as *merging with* and not *subsumed by* his identity. Hilda's divorce-related jealousy is a genuine discontinuity in her own self-identity. She is not merely obsessed, possessive, dependent, or suffering from any other form of territoriality. Hilda truly loved. She does not deserve to be taunted for feeling jealous nor, of course, encouraged to practice jealousy as a sort of perverse virtue. She is experiencing what she feels she must, what is unforgivingly inevitable in cases such as Hilda's. Hilda is haunted by the feeling she is living with but a remnant of her former self. This feeling is not unique to Hilda. In fact, this feeling is so common Count Leo Tolstoy captured it vividly in his novel, *Anna Karenina*. Anna's tragedy lies in the fact she is never able to muster the courage to deal with the feeling. Eventually, she gives up all hope of acquiring an appropriate sense of self. It is no surprise to the reader when Anna commits suicide. With no sense of self, a body becomes just one more inconvenience.

Genuine erotic love is wonderful stuff, but it involves real risk. In cases of real love, divorce destroys that which is most ennobling in human beings' *uncompromising union*. The destruction of erotic love through divorce may be the single most devastating psychological experience common to humankind, save the death of a spouse or child.

Jealousy, as an expression of territoriality, can be a very intense emotion, yet it is one most people overcome. The jealousy of erotic love is much more difficult to manage since it is a defining characteristic of an individual's self-concept. Perhaps the best one can do in such cases is learn to live with it as Hilda does: "I pretend he's dead." She does not burden her future with hopes of a reunion. Neither does she plague it with the futile hope of forgetting all that is past. Divorce scars. The attacks of the furies are the cause of the scars. For those who suffer from the scarring of shattered erotic love, the scarring may never heal.

Grief

Grief is the easiest of the furies to describe. Though no less destructive than the other furies, the grief of divorce is similar to the grief experienced on the heels of nearly any tragedy. Grief is a form of emotional exhaustion generally precipitated by explicitly identifiable events. This makes grief substantively different from the mood of depression which is a less agitated state and reflects the general and often indiscriminate erosion of psychological resiliency. As John, a forty-four-year old professor, divorcing for the second time, put it:

> It's as if divorce causes an explosion of all sorts of bad emotions in your life. When everything external simmers down you just feel bad... real bad, and confused, real confused.

People know divorce frees the furies from their Pandora's Box, but knowledge does not prevent people from being victimized by them. When a person feels there is no fight left in him or her, that person is exposed to the merciless wrath of one or more of the furies. After the other furies have sufficiently brutalized the divorcee, then grief begins its reign. If the reign of grief lingers for long, the end result may be clinical depression. Grief is unavoidable but need not be sustained for long. As long as the divorcee is unwilling to surrender to the attack of the other furies, grief can be kept at bay.

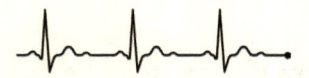

5

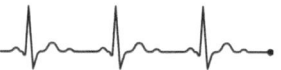

The Victory

Once the divorce is finalized, there is no choice but to live with it. When the gavel sounds and the judge enters the decree, the divorce becomes a matter of legal record and social fact. To have made it so far without suffering any major physical or emotional illness is not much of a victory, though some naively believe it to be so. Whether you have successfully traversed the trauma of divorce and whether you have begun the adventure of creating a new life are questions still begging for answers at this point. For many people, the granting of the divorce decree is anti-climactic. If division of property and custody have been worked out, the lawyers alone may appear in court on behalf of their clients. Divorcees who accompany their lawyers in so-called uncontested proceedings find the experience one of great humiliation as Kathy, a businesswoman in her mid-thirties explained:

> I went to court with my lawyer just to make sure there would be no last-minute shenanigans. Also, I thought it would be symbolic of putting an ugly part of my life behind me and beginning a new, happier life. (My girlfriends also planned to take

me out after work to celebrate my "new life.") It turned out to be one of the most humiliating experiences of my life. You're crammed into a room with a horde of people. There seems to be a lack of self-esteem, contempt and anger wherever you look. You wait until your name is called, and then you walk to the judge's bench with your lawyer and bang, it's all over. It's like a cattle call, processing the tragedy of human failure.

Of course, in a contested divorce, the hearing tends to exhaust the participants—regardless of the outcome. In short, the granting of the decree is rarely a watershed. At best, it marks the passage of time confirming the couple's original falling out. At worst, it may forebode more harm is yet to come. If you have gone through the divorce process, grasping for scraps of a life long since passed, the granting of the divorce may set you reeling with the knowledge you are alone, all alone. This realization delays the start of post-divorce recovery for many divorcees. The mere passage of time sets no one on the road to a new or healthier lifestyle. For that, you need to take conscious control of your lifestyle and begin creating your own destiny. The road to post-divorce recovery begins when the divorcee decides to start planning for success and then acts in accord with sensible, well-made plans.

Every divorcee confronts the furies. So, too, every divorcee must rebuild an appropriate lifestyle, a lifestyle free of the furies. You cannot rebuild a lifestyle in a day. Like any war or physical competition, there are preparations to be made, battles to be fought, campaigns to be waged, points to be scored. Unlike an actual war or physical campaign, victory over divorce does not occur with the drama of a surrender at Appomattox. The divorcee may experience several false victories before he or she realizes anything truly substantive. Divorcees often conclude the effects of the divorce are all in the past only to discover the furies waiting again in ambush. Nevertheless, for most, a day will come when victory is achieved. Even when victory is achieved, it usually takes another few months before the divorcee realizes the war is over. The war may be over and victory complete, but the savvy divorcee knows the terrain of his or her life has been changed forever.

The divorcee's new life may be extraordinarily rewarding. What it cannot be is identical to pre-divorce life. One can no more recover the innocence of the never-divorced any more than one can recover one's youth. Nevertheless, good things are possible. For example, in achieving victory over divorce, some people become physically fit—perhaps for the first time in their lives. They may acquire a strength and endurance far surpassing anything realized in their youth. Fitness makes most people feel like a new beginning is dawning on the horizon. The fear of lost years is replaced with a sense of excitement. The divorcee discovers new confidence in his or her ability to meet physical and mental stress head on.

Millions of unexceptional people get divorced and somehow muddle through the rest of their lives with no divorce-related morbid event. This, too, is a victory, albeit a small one. The goal should not be just to muddle through. People only get one shot at life, so they should try to make as much of it as they can. The goal should be to luxuriate in life and not just endure it.

How long does it take to create a new life, free of the ravages of the furies, of destructive divorce-related habits, and melancholy memories? Most psychologists claim it takes two years to get over a divorce. However, other researchers argue a more realistic figure is half the time the couple was married. My personal experience has shown me one can recover from the dissolution of a sixteen-year marriage in as few as six months. To do so, one must desire it and pursue the following recommendations:

1. **Fight back** — *When confronting divorce, fight back with honor.*

    - Recognize that you are your own worst enemy.

    - Be as objective as possible in dividing property and making arrangements for custody.

    - Select a lawyer who will work for you and who accepts your commitment to maintaining a sense of honor and self-respect.

2. **Exercise** — *If you already exercise, do more. If you don't, start.*

    - Aerobic exercise is a must: This includes things like running, swimming, walking, an exercise class, and cycling. It will protect your physiology from the ravages of stress and help enhance your psychological well-being.

    - Anaerobic exercise can help, too. This includes things like weight lifting and sprints. It is the kind of exercise that tones muscles and produces definition. The psychological boost of seeing new muscle again is immeasurable.

3. **Diet** — *Watch what you eat.*

- Control: Putting yourself on a Spartan-like diet is an important way of taking control of your life. For many, it is the first step toward building a new lifestyle.

- Nutrition: You eat to build good health NOT to lose or gain weight. Good food will protect your body from stress and keep your mind in keen form.

4. **Confront the Furies** — *They won't give up without a fight.*

    - Realize the attack of the furies is inevitable and universal. You are not unique in this. Your spouse, too, will confront the full range of furies. Be the first in your divorce to wage a successful campaign against the furies.

    - Identify the fury or set of furies attacking you at any given moment. By focusing on the character and intensity of each fury as it occurs, you will be better able to confront it.

5. **Target the furies** — *You can outscore them.*

    - **Guilt:** Assign guilt generously to each partner in turn, and then REALIZE these are no longer important issues to resolve.

    - **Hate:** Is this person, deed, policy, or habit something you can reasonably expect to obliterate from your world without incurring further guilt or some other fury? If not, then REALIZE this is an emotion without a point!

- **Anger:** What makes you indignant? What are the chances of exacting appropriate compensation? Make a plan to exact whatever compensation is due you without making yourself vulnerable to further guilt, fear, grief, or hate. If there is no reasonable expectation for exacting just compensation, then REALIZE this divorce-related emotion no longer has a point in your life.

6. **Fear**

    - **Acute fear (Panic):** Do not run. Do whatever it is you set out to do when the panic attack occurred. If you suspect genuine physical problems may be present, then see your doctor. Explain the circumstance of the attacks and that you are going through a divorce. If the attacks continue despite your knowledge you are in no serious physical danger, seek professional psychological help IMMEDIATELY.

    - **Chronic Fear:** Worries that you will die alone, never find another, or survive by yourself can be alleviated by planning the life you choose to live as a single person.

7. **Jealousy**

    - **Territorial Imperative:** Ask yourself, "What value to me is there in claiming a property right over this person? Does this person represent property I rightfully exercise control over?" After recognizing that "none" and "no" are, respectively, the answers to these questions, REALIZE you cannot exercise property claims over another person. This tendency is quite primitive and, consequently, beneath you.

- **The Dissolution of Erotic Love:** Accept the fact you shared a beautiful project together. If the person had died, this project would have been just as beautiful and just as (un)finished. Your former erotic love can always be a source of beautiful memories. But just as if your spouse had died, you must live on. If you were a partner in an erotic love, remember you want your partner to be happy and your partner would want you to be happy. Consequently, your task now is to find new happiness. This is a rare and difficult challenge, but if you once found erotic love, you have already proven yourself to be a rare and special person uniquely capable of understanding this sort of thing.

8. **Grief**

    - Confront the accompanying furies bringing grief into your life. Without them, grief cannot exist.

    - Make a plan for building a new lifestyle. Along the way this will cause you to adopt a new more optimistic world-view.

    - Begin acting on the plan you are constructing for a new life as a single.

    - Consider keeping a diary in which you record each small success in your recovery. In print, cheer your own achievements and laugh at your failures.

By working on these recommendations, you can begin your recovery while still suffering the early stages of divorce. To successfully complete your recovery, much will depend on how you expect to live your life as a single, your plan for making single life appealing and, finally, how aggressive you are in acting in accord with those plans.

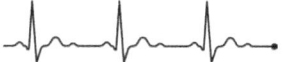

Epilogue — Part I

The point of this book is to bring you from the throes of divorce to the advent of a new life in less time than experts predict is normal. Nevertheless, unless you are a very, very, very slow reader, you will be able to read this book from cover to cover in less time than it takes to recover from divorce.

Remember, this is a book covering an entire range of adult experience. You need to move through your recovery as systematically and deliberately as possible. Below is a spectrum representing the experiences explored in Part I of this book. If you find yourself anywhere on the continuum, then go back to that section of the book and begin reading again. Take your time. Meditate on what is being said and on the stories of others. If you no longer find yourself situated anywhere along the spectrum below, then you are ready to read the chapters in Part II.

PART 1

The Announce-ment	The Initial Onslaught of the Furies	Apart and Opposed	Fight	Keeping Control	The Furies distiguish themselves	Victory	Hereafter
• Shock • Void • Emptiness • Confusion	• Tangled emotions all rushing in at once OR a feeling of relief... clouded with moments of grave doubt.	• Recognizing the adversarial nature of court proceedings.	• Search for self-respect. • Potential loss of honor. • Quest for moral balance.	• Defend yourself from yourself • Remember your lawyer works for you - keep control of your case.	• You have met each of the furies. • You have seen them race at you in pairs and triplets. • You have felt their tenaciousness.	• The furies are confounded by your strength. • You know you have met the enemy and you have WON!	• Where do you go from here?

PART II

Post Divorce

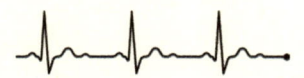

6

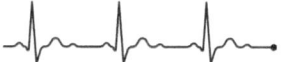

Waxing Philosophical

What is the point of life?
Does my life have any value?
Do I matter in this world?

People often ask these questions upon the heels of great calamity. The calamity may be a death in the family, loss of a job, becoming a victim of serious crime, a major illness or an accident. For people who are particularly high strung, it may be something as trivial as turning forty; for others, it may be divorce.

Everyone has occasion sometime during life to wax philosophical, to consider questions each believes will give direction to his or her life. People do this often as children and again as adolescents. For example, at the beginning of adult life, it seems important to distinguish the kind of person one is becoming from the kind one *ought* to become. It is a matter of getting a sense of direction in creating or revising a life plan and then following it.

Regardless of how well-made the plans, in some areas at least, people always drift wide of the mark. For example, if marriage was once a part of one's life plan then one expected any marriage to last a lifetime. Surely no one would go to the trouble of getting married if he or she thought the enterprise was destined to failure. Divorce tears asunder the integrity and consistency of a life plan, and it does so in traumatic fashion.

For the most part, once people are into the adult years, they pay little attention to life plans. They just act. Adults pay bills, seek job promotions, clean house, seek new means of entertainment, pay taxes, raise kids, shop... where is there any time for assessing how nearly one is fulfilling a LIFE PLAN? The disparity between one's current life-style and a long-ago formed life plan can seem enormous. At a time of crisis one may wail, "Where did I go wrong? I had all these wonderful plans, so what happened?"

Existential writers, such as Jean Paul Sartre, believe such laments represent unsurpassed opportunities. They cause a person to realize people are separate from the world of mere things.

Too many people, particularly those subject to unwanted divorce, see themselves as nothing more than a toppling domino in a grand design. On the other hand, the divorcee who sees herself or himself as apart from the world is uninhibited by such forlorn suspicions. These people see the uncertainties of the future as ripe with possibilities, each responsive to human willfulness. *The world defines the context in which a person lives, but the person decides how to act within that context.* As the existentialist warns, the stuff of the world is not sympathetic to our *dreams*. Still, the world, and even the people in it, are responsive to our *deeds*. The world each person experiences is as much a world of his or her making as it is a world containing one's actions.

The world cannot drive a person away from a chosen life plan. It only presents the context in which a life plan is implemented. Most things interrupting a life plan are under the control of the individual and can be remediated. Things such as careless imagination limit prospects for future happiness far more than the changing physical features of the world.

The recovering divorcee needs to examine the circumstances in which he or she lives. Such things as health, age, environment, sex, geographical location, familial responsibilities, job, financial resources, education, and personality traits each influence how the individual ought to act. The point of action is to move away from the doldrums of divorce and towards an active search for alloying distractions and increasing happiness.

Life is for making, not for lamenting. The best lives are lived. They are lived by people who are conscientious about pursuing actions which have value, which is determined by feelings of being more "real," being "good," being "important," being "focused," experiencing a sense of "vividness" and more.

Waxing philosophical about life's value is no idle pastime for the recently divorced. Quite the contrary. It constitutes the preliminary planning sending one ahead towards a future of his or her own making.

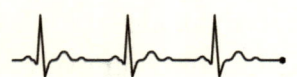

7

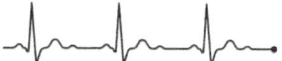

From Loneliness to Aloneness

Sunday nights turned out to be a time of great disappointment in my new life as a single. While married, my weekends were always a flurry of activity. However, on Sunday nights, the whole family gathered about in the living room, ate a light dinner, and watched the Walt Disney show. As a single person, Sunday nights were the time I was most acutely aware of how alone I was.

It had been years since I had been so alone, and this stark sense of aloneness quickly degenerated into loneliness. Throughout the work week there was much to do, much to distract me from the fact I no longer had a family to go home to. Even on weekends, long after I established a comfortable social schedule, Sunday evenings struck me as a lonely time. Surrounded by the works of Plato, Kant, Einstein, and Sartre, a briefcase full of student papers to grade, newly made friends to call, I sat on Sunday nights feeling alone and uncomfortable. More often than not, I would turn on my five-inch screen black and white television (usually for the first time all week) and watch Walt Disney. I went to bed shortly thereafter and hoped for sleep to bring Monday morning as quickly as possible.

The rituals of married life do not disappear simultaneously with the signing of a decree. A fellow divorcee, Connie, confided for months after her divorce she felt silly and self-conscious about her sadness. She felt sad each Friday night because her husband was no longer coming home. Her sadness made her feel silly because ever since they were married, every Friday night he was always drunk. "He may have been drunk," she said, "but he was always jovial, full of apologies and pleading for my pardon." She was happy she no longer had to deal with his irresponsible behavior. Still, she was peculiarly uncomfortable knowing he was not coming home at all. The recollections made her feel lonely. Being free of her dependent past did not free her *for* happiness.

The abrupt end of family rituals, both good and bad, may provoke the deepest feelings of loneliness. Any sharing of lives erodes the boundaries people normally fix around them. This is true of college roommates as well as bunkmates in a military barracks. It is especially true of lovers and, most of all, spouses. The initial loneliness of divorce is the loneliness of boundary-less persons, people accustomed to at least one relationship where boundaries are kept to a minimum.

The need to maintain boundaries at all times after divorce is a very odd feeling. One thirty-seven-year old woman, Ruth, said, "Imagine the feeling you would have if you were wholly alone in a public place and were stark naked! No one can see you, but the experience is such an affront to your sense of protocol it is very difficult to become accustomed to it. You'd rather not be here under these conditions, and that is how I feel about single life."

Take away the shared rituals and add uncertainty about who will be around the next time there's an illness or some other unpredictable tragedy and the loneliness of divorce intensifies. When this occurs, most divorcee see being alone as a bad or, at least, threatening experience. Loneliness and being alone become for them one and the same experience. An important milestone for every divorcee is learning that *being alone* need not be accompanied by feelings of loneliness.

The feeling of loneliness, abandoned rituals and a boundary-full existence may be intensified by intimate and familiar surroundings. The most potent of these is typically THE HOUSE. An expression many divorcees are fond of using is, "The house remains full of ghosts." Their point is the house and its contents evoke feelings and memories of the previous marriage. Good and bad memories blend together as a constant reminder that "alone" accurately describes one's social status. Under such circumstances, it is difficult to learn being alone need not mean being lonely.

Divorcees must learn their *aloneness* can be a catalyst for new opportunities. Aloneness is a condition of freedom. With no one else to depend upon, the successful divorcee learns to become self-reliant and then to flourish.

Living alone can be a spectacular though rarely appreciated adventure. Knowing you are prepared to meet any challenge leads to a kind of euphoria. Unfortunately, too few people experience it.

The divorcee can also choose to treat it as a self-imposed prison, a choice made usually because the divorcee can't imagine how to exploit the freedom afforded to a person living alone. Living alone successfully doesn't come easily. It is something that must be learned and few Americans ever had the opportunity to learn it. For many Americans, life is comprised by a nearly endless stream of roommates.

The prototype roommate situation is the immediate family. Families nurture the young. The best families raise children who become responsible as adults and able to share with others.

Many families fall short of that mark however.

Some families abuse children. Abused children are desperately dependent on each moment of good will afforded them by their parents. These children often grow into adults who cling to personal relationships because they sense it represents the closest thing to happiness. The formerly abused child may, as an adult, regard his or her dependent actions as a show of commitment but, in effect, the person's partner is likely to regard the actions as self-serving and parasitic.

For example, consider the following account of a couple married for five years prior to their divorce. Linda was a raven-haired beauty with a well-toned figure that called to mind the sex symbols of the 1950s. Eric was a medical doctor, whose appearance reminded one of the rugged good looks of actor Channing Tatum. When they divorced, he was twenty-six and she was twenty-two. They were an extremely attractive couple and both claimed the spouse as a "best friend" and "lover" during their courting. Both of Linda's parents had been alcoholics. They died at an early age of alcohol-related illnesses. Eric's father was much older than his mother. This was his second marriage. Eric's mother was very dependent on her husband's leadership. Linda explained:

> After a few years Eric just started taking me for granted. I suppose it was that medical school sort of thing. Young medical student chased after by pretty nurses. Because I loved him and knew he was going through a stressful period in his life, I tried to look the other way. I fixed his meals, took care of the apartment, worked at a grocery store, did anything he wanted sexually. I did everything I could and yet nothing seemed adequate. Sure, there were times I would blow up. I needed at-

tention. All he would do is tell me how important everything else in his life was at the time. He just became selfish and self-centered. I pity the next girl Eric marries.

In contrast, Eric lamented:

Linda was great. I'll probably always love her, in part. But she drove me crazy. She was constantly asking me to tell her how much I loved her. She wanted me to tell her how to behave at work, at home and even how to have sex. Here I was just trying to keep my own life together and she's trying to get me to live her life as well! It was terribly draining. I was exhausted at work, and I just couldn't face going home. I thought things would get better after I graduated, but they never did. If I wasn't telling her how much I loved her, how to live or how happy I was that she let me make all "our" decisions, she would berate me for not caring. Even when I started messing around with other women, she was still the one I loved. I just couldn't be with her. In a sense, you might say it was she who made it impossible for us to be together. She was like a leech, sucking away all my strength. I never did understand why she got that way.

Within months after the divorce, Linda met and married a local rock and roll singer who never completed high school. Three years later Eric had still not re-married.

In this situation, Linda saw herself as giving everything to "the relationship" while Eric saw her as parasitic. Both saw Linda as being overly zealous at times, and both recognized Eric had drifted away. What seemed to start as a perfect relationship fell apart because neither party knew how to live together with another.

Linda had lived with her parents until she and Eric married. Because both her parents were alcoholic, Linda believed herself to be very independent: "From the time I got into high school, my brother and I could never depend on our parents, so we just took care of each other and raised ourselves." Linda and her brother had been beaten by their parents, but since the family lived in a relatively expensive house and the children dressed in stylish clothes, spent lavish sums of money and were active in the school's extra-curricular activities, no one suspected abuse.

Eric lived with his parents until moving in with fraternity brothers in college. Linda's experience led her to believe intimacy required dependency and desperate intensity. Eric's previous experience led him to believe intimacy was a matter of casual sharing. He was not prepared for the intensity sought by Linda. Eric was unprepared to give what Linda required. Linda was unprepared to recognize Eric's persistent desire for autonomy. Neither of the partners were prepared for adopting a common life plan.

Would living together before marriage have helped? Perhaps, but current research suggests otherwise. People who live together before marrying are more likely to divorce than those who marry without any prior co-habitation. Psychologists believe living together deludes people into thinking they can make a go of it when, actually, it distracts them from the crucial features of commitment. Commitment, in the sense required by marriage, means two people intend to address the world as one family unit. Living together requires only one hold up his or her end of the bargain much the way one is expected to do in a business partnership. Just as in a business, if the going gets rough one can always sell out and look for more fruitful investments. Indeed, as in a business partnership, there is no reason why one cannot seek or solicit other "investment opportunities" while enjoying the fruits of a thriving *partnership*.

Marriage requires a very special sort of "roommate" relationship. In marriage, two independent people choose to act in the best interests of the other. The roommate relationship of most young people shields them from developing an appropriate sense of independence and from distinguishing between the bonding of marriage and that required simply to "hang out together." Linda saw marriage as a license to appropriate Eric's will. Eric saw marriage as an agreement to share expenses and remain the "best of buddies." When it became evident to each the other saw things differently, Eric and Linda each began adding up the unfairness of the relationship. This spelled doom for two roommates attempting a marriage.

Marriage requires an unqualified sense of giving on the part of both spouses. When this is lacking, one or both partners may begin auditing the flow of give and take. As soon as either spouse begins keeping a ledger detailing what he or she has given to the relationship, the relationship deteriorates.

Marriage traffics in much which is intangible. It is well near impossible for two people to evaluate, objectively, the respective contributions of either. The attempt to audit a relationship forces the auditor to imagine he or she is outside the relationship looking in. While this may be an advisable practice when negotiating a divorce, it is inadvisable in sustaining a marriage. Marriage is to be lived from within. One can no more give an account of how to balance the books with a mate than a hand can grasp itself. Marriage is meant to move forward without the tentativeness or wheeling dealing of commercial relationships.

This is not the spirit of "It's you and me against the world until death do us part."

Marriages thrive by being lived and not by spouses antiseptically observing and judging the relative merits of their mate's efforts. If one accepts the other as a soulmate for life, what is to be gained by insisting one gets one's share? In a well-working family unit, anything one contributes to the family benefits each member. In other words, the ability to share unreservedly is the crucial element in commitment. This is something that cannot be gotten at by merely living together. The roommate experience cannot serve as an apt model for the challenges of marriage.

Most people's previous living arrangements afford little opportunity for learning what amounts to complete and unconstrained sharing. In childhood, power and responsibility are unevenly distributed. As a result, children look at their parent's marriage "from the outside." In ideal cases, children may see parents sharing, but this is no guarantee the child will move to the next step and understand or *feel what it means to share,* rather than merely co-operate. In the worst cases, there may be neither sharing between peers nor concern for dependents. College or work-related roommates require very little of each other. Once bargains are struck, roommates only ask the other to stick to his or her end of the deal. There is no need for unconstrained sharing.

To be able to share in an unconstrained way, you need to know yourself. Only then can you recognize when you are giving of yourself as opposed to seeking fulfillment of personal wants.

To share intimately, you need also to know your partner. Consider, for example, what you would give to the person who had everything; the answer... nothing. You can only give effectively to a person who has real needs and desires you understand.

The aloneness divorce brings is often the first real opportunity people have for coming to learn about themselves. Those who exploit this opportunity make better marriage partners the second time around. Statistics indicate second marriages among people who have been divorced for two or more years show a surprising resiliency. As long as one is plagued with fears that being alone is tantamount to loneliness, that person will never learn what he or she has to share with another.

Lonely people are not selfish. Selfishness is a matter of deliberately setting one's own interests ahead of others. Lonely people do not mean to be selfish. In fact, they are often quite giving. They may be parasitic, but they are not selfish. Lonely people cannot share because they are too egocentric. Despite intentions to the contrary, their egocentrism focuses their attention on their loneliness and away from the fact they can survive alone. Moreover, their fears keep them from learning they can be good company.

No one truly gives at the same time he or she is desperately taking from others. Loving relationships are built around people giving to, and not taking from, the building of a common project. Lonely people do not understand this fact about relationships. As a consequence, they are less likely to connect with others. Their loneliness tends to sustain the experience they most fear.

Nearly everyone who gets divorced feels lonely. But before entering into a new relationship, you must move away from loneliness and towards the realization that learning to be happy while alone is a pre-requisite for loving in the future.

Loving relationships require two independent people join together *interdependently* to seek the fulfillment of a common set of needs and interests. There are no back doors and no shortcuts out of, or away from, loneliness and onward towards shared happiness. If a divorcee seeks intimacy just to avoid loneliness, then his or her goal is not to share with another but rather to exploit the other's strengths and resources. Independent people, too, have needs, but they know they can muddle through and survive. If they join with another, it is not from fear of loneliness but from optimistic respect for what each wants to do for the other.

Finally, the stark reality is the older a person is when re-entering the single world, the more likely the person is to stay single for life. This is particularly true for women due to the death rates for men, the disproportionate number of men incarcerated or employed in occupations making courtship improbable, and the long-standing preference of older men for younger women (and younger women for older men). Since a single life-style is a real possibility for *any divorcee*, it only makes sense one should learn to live alone and thrive alone. The future may be spent alone. It is best it not feel lonely as well.

Lessons to be Learned by the Recently Divorced

1. Use your alone time to learn about yourself.
2. Avoid co-dependent romances (you are particularly vulnerable to these shortly after your or the other's divorce).
3. Be cautious of romances with people who are intensely *lonely*.
4. Seek others who, like yourself, have found fulfillment while alone.

8

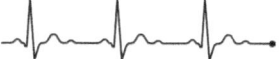

Wonderment

Just as learning to be alone leads naturally to self-discovery, so too, self-discovery leads to wonderment. Through self-discovery, the divorcee is freed from the totems previously depended upon for self-identity: the BMW and thousand-dollar business suit become less important; the turtleneck sweater, herringbone coat, and armful of books are no longer necessary for strolling across campus in professional style. The uncomfortable high-heeled shoes and outrageously-priced designer clothes may be scoffed at as pretentious, unbecoming, and unnecessary for a liberated career woman. And finally, in contrast to all the above, the sweatshirt-clad housewife who served as the always smiling chauffeur for a station wagon full of rug rats may, after divorce, opt for skirts, heels, a Lexus, and time to jog.

For many married people, the range of what matters and what is possible, shrinks each year. There is good and bad to this. On the one hand, the routines of marriage contribute to a longer and healthier life for most people because routines relieve stress. Appropriate decision-making routines augment the building of joint life projects. Routines help ensure resources are expended for mutual benefit. Admittedly, some routines accumulate for no particular purpose at all. Purposeless routines can erode a couple's sense of fun and adventure.

When a divorcee learns he or she is freed from unnecessary routines, the realization can be exhilarating. It is like being twenty-two-years old and believing the world is just waiting for you to change it. Happily, unlike twenty-two-year-olds, middle-aged people are much better at exploiting the opportunities the world has to offer than are their younger counterparts. Divorcees typically have fewer expendable dollars than when they were married but usually a whole lot more than when they were twenty-two. They are well poised for new adventure.

Admittedly, there are limitations to what you can do. A forty-six-year old overweight man cannot seriously plan a successful career as a defensive end in the NFL. On the other hand, he can lose weight. He can jog, lift weights, bicycle, swim, give up alcohol, do triathlons, go dancing, work a few more hours each day, and still play more than he ever did before. Similarly, the portly, graying former housewife will not be auditioned for the lead in a professional performance of *Swan Lake*. She can, however, dye her hair, take up aerobics, go to college, start a career, dance, join the local chapter of the Sierra Club, take up scuba diving, or even ask a man for a date. In short, she can try the world on in a thousand and one different ways. There is enough excitement out there for everyone. Not even money matters very much. Imagine any income level and then think of all the things people in that income level can do. Few people have done little of what their economic and social surroundings would allow.

Wonderment also excites the ambition. The divorced police officer may go to law school. The waitress may go to college and study accounting. One forty-six-year old doctor, an orthopedic surgeon, gave up his very lucrative practice and returned to the family farm. He now rides a tractor from dawn till dusk, does mechanical repair around the farm and, on weekends, dances with the girls at a local road house. In another case, a New York stockbroker returned to college at the age of thirty-three to get a teaching certificate. He met a girl from the country (quite different from his former wife, a very cosmopolitan journalist) and opened a tourist home near her girlhood home. And, finally, there was the woman who worked as a laboratory technician, who drove a dilapidated economy car for nearly eight years during her marriage. After her divorce, she went to medical school. After graduation, she bought a Mercedes and now leads a very active social life centered around the performing arts. In each of these cases, the people discovered a life plan dramatically different from what he or she had previously endured.

The middle-aged crazies plague those who believe they have little control over their lives. They feel there is nothing more to discover about themselves. In contrast, people who are accustomed to being alone learn they are free to sculpt a life uniquely suited to their individual tastes. Before this begins sounding too Pollyanna-ish, remember, self-discovery leads only to an understanding of who you are—not to the acquisition of everything you fancy. It is tempting after a divorce to wallow in a fit of Hollywood/Madison Avenue-governed whimsy. This is not the same thing as discovering the world anew. The experience of wonderment leads you to consider *where you fit* in this world and shows you the prospects for a happy life can be very, very good.

Part of what lies ahead typically involves engaging in new relationships. What type of person best suits the new you, the real you? The only way to find out is to begin dating. Dating shortly after divorce accomplishes two things. First, it reminds you you are a sexual and social being who did not die when the marriage failed. There are members of the opposite sex who will find comfort and joy in your company. Second, dating gives you a chance to find out more about yourself. Date people from many walks of life and with as varied interests as possible. Your initial purpose in dating after a divorce is not to find another life partner. Rather, it is to find out what sort of personalities and world-views are most attractive to you and who are most attracted to you. Along the way, you will be goaded into trying activities you thought better left alone, activities beyond your financial means, or your athletic ability, activities seemingly uninteresting or, perhaps, too dangerous. Some of these activities will catch your attention so you will henceforth become an enthusiast, others will not. Nevertheless, the ones that do capture your imagination will more than make up for the time and money expended on those which do not.

In my own case, I had long been a runner. Through my association with a multi-talented athletic woman, I found myself looking forward to long distance bike rides on Sundays, participating in biathlons (an event combining running and biking) and pushing myself to complete my first marathon. These activities became an essential part of my life as did opera. The association with the person who introduces you to new pleasures may dissolve, but you learn your interests and leisure activities are more enriching and varied than anything you previously imagined.

If learning to be alone is the beginning of a successful and full recovery from divorce, then wonderment is the catalyst for flourishing as a single person. Wonderment is not a gift to those favored by the gods. You make wonderment happen by *doing*. If you wait to be inspired, little may happen. On the other hand, you can act now and discover inspiration follows naturally.

Making Wonderment Happen

Assuming you no longer fear loneliness and can enjoy being alone, try some new activities:

1. Begin formal lessons to learn a new sport.
2. Join a special interest group or charity such as the Sierra Club or local Cancer Society.
3. Take formal courses in several different fields both to broaden your interests and to help you consider the plausibility of a career change.
4. For those with children, Parents Without Partners or some similar church-related group can be helpful.
5. Go to social functions you never considered previously. Get online. Read the entertainment section of the local newspapers to learn what activities are offered in and around your town.
6. Date a variety of people. Do not regard these liaisons as the potential beginning of new romance. If you are recently divorced, most people will understand you are not emotionally or intellectually prepared for romance. You are out to have a good time and learn what it means to enjoy the company of other people, *casually*, on a one on one basis.

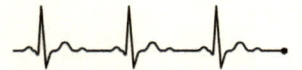

9

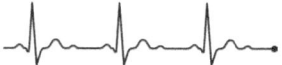

Escaping the Pitfalls

Whether or not one enters a state of wonderment after divorce, you will, by necessity, find a context within which to begin living the rest of your life. Establishing a post-divorce life-style is a rather bumpy affair. Learning to be alone and enjoying the experience of wonderment is typically achieved only after much effort. In finding a home for one's future life-style, most people succumb to several predictable pitfalls. Until people pass beyond these pitfalls, it is impossible for them to experience the joys of wonderment.

The four most common pitfalls hindering divorcees in their quest for wonderment and self-discovery are chemical dependency, workaholism, reclusiveness, and promiscuity. A person may fall victim to one or more of these after divorce. These pitfalls are so common because each comes very close to a task one ought, or inevitably feels compelled, to engage in after divorce. It is the excessive or indelicate pursuit of each or several of these tasks that results in their becoming dangerous entrapments for the individual. And to make matters worse, it is not always clear which pitfall will be most ensnaring in the life of any individual or which combination of pitfalls will handicap the recovery of the divorcee. For example, a person who is reclusive may, in addition, develop a drinking problem. If not resolved immediately, the imprudent use of alcohol can destroy the person's health, while reclusiveness continues to erode the divorcee's psychological well-being. In fact, a person may appear to be a workaholic when, in effect, the person has retreated from personal contact with others by throwing him or herself into an independent work project. In other words, to the observer, the divorcee may appear to be entangled in one pitfall when actually the greatest threat is from a combination of problems or a less evident but far deeper problem area.

Substance Abuse

Chemical dependency is the most dangerous syndrome potentially confronting the divorcee. Divorcees may become reclusive, finding solace in the bottom of a bottle night after night. On the other hand, divorcees may throw themselves into what they take to be the swinging singles scene. Night after night they hit the singles bars… and drink. Some drink simply to imitate the behavior of others around them. Others drink to muster courage to approach members of the opposite sex or to appear more approachable. Whatever the reason, divorcees and the bar scene tend to be a lethal combination. For example, insurance data indicates in the first year after a divorce, there is a statistically significant increase in the likelihood a divorcee will be involved in an accident. Moreover (and much to the dismay of insurance companies), alcohol is usually reported as a contributing factor in the accident. The occurrence of alcohol-related accidents is so prevalent among recent divorcees it has motivated insurance companies to explore the legality of identifying divorce as a risk factor when determining insurance rates. In short, alcohol and the recently divorced are an unhappy, though somewhat common, combination.

    Chemical dependency is not restricted to alcohol. If the recently divorced moved in groups where cocaine or marijuana were occasionally used as social stimulants, their use of these chemicals is likely to increase following the divorce as well. On a less exotic level, there are many divorcees who find the process of divorce unmanageable. They go to their family doctor complaining about vague symptoms, and in the course of the examination, they let on they are in the process of divorce. Well-meaning doctors often conclude the divorcee is wrestling with a "bad case of nerves." Subsequently, they prescribe a tranquilizer to help the patient over transient difficult times. Once the tranquilizers are in the hands of the patient, the patient's use of the substance is largely out of the physician's control. Chemical dependency is potentially lurking about in all such cases. Even to those who find the indiscreet use of alcohol abhorrent, the use of doctor-prescribed medicine may seem far less offensive. Furthermore, one may reason, if one tranquilizer takes the edge off things, two may bring about genuine relaxation, and three may bring about peace and much-desired sleep. In rather short order, the divorcee may discover "medicine" can banish anxiety from the forefront of his or her consciousness. As in the case of alcohol abuse, the *solution* is short-lived and serves only to create more severe problems in the long run.

    No social, professional or economic status is immune from the pitfalls of chemical dependency following a divorce. For example, one psychologist related the following personal account:

I'm a clinical psychologist. I know the problems people have when going through a divorce. I was determined to use my knowledge and avoid the problems other lay-types trouble themselves with. Being Jewish, I rarely drink. Sometimes a bit of wine with a meal—particularly a meal of religious significance. In any case, I started having a glass of wine each night with dinner. You know, to sort of wind-down from a day of listening to other people's problems (when I have problems of my own!). Soon, I was having a glass of wine when arriving at home, another at dinner and one while watching the ten o'clock news. Before long, I was drinking a bottle of wine each day and then I started drinking cocktails after work as well. After six months, I started developing health problems, and I knew if I didn't stop drinking, I was going to have some major problems.

The whole time I never had a date. I'd work, come home and drink. I was just tired of women and tired of being me. It took me a couple of years to get over it. I'm dating a woman now and things are okay. I don't know if I ever want to get married again. I'm just suspicious of women—scratch that—other persons. I don't want to get hurt again, and I know how vulnerable I am to the same dangers I try to counsel others away from.

Knowing full-well chemical dependency is a common problem for the recently divorced, this professionally-trained Ph.D. in clinical psychology still found himself slipping into the dangerous routines that plagued his clients. This is all the more astonishing when one recalls the psychologist was very nearly a tee-totaler prior to divorce. Readers of Thomas Maedor's *Children of Psychiatrists* may not find this astonishing since Maedor's evidence suggests psychiatrists, psychologists and other psychotherapists tend to be more commonly afflicted by, or at least vulnerable to, psychological imbalances than the public at large. Still, the public at large continues to believe, as a class, these professionals are free from the foibles plaguing other mere mortals. However, the facts are to the contrary. Appropriate knowledge, social position and prior clean-living are not sufficient for avoiding post-divorce pitfalls.

A nurse and hospital administrator, directing several research projects for one of the country's leading medical schools, became drug dependent after her divorce despite knowing firsthand the dangers of addiction. She was divorcing her successful, attorney husband because he was addicted to cocaine.

> I can't believe I let myself get caught up in the use of drugs as a crutch. While married, I would have an occasional drink at social events and that was all. After my divorce, dating became common and as a result I found myself having two or three drinks several times each week. At night, I had to gear down from either work or social activities. I had to get my sleep. I would occasionally take a valium to help me sleep. I knew the dangers of mixing valium and alcohol but, nevertheless, I just found my use of both spiraling. Finally, I found myself making embarrassing errors at work. And I was emotionally distressed at night. I was becoming increasingly concerned that the men I went out with liked me - even if I didn't care for them. In any case, one Friday night, I was home alone reflecting on my plight and I just decided I had to clean

up my life. So for the past three months, I haven't had more than two or three glasses of wine and no valium. I also go out far less often, worry less about whether or not I "am liked" and find that my dates are now much more fun.

Not everyone can abruptly change their habituation to substance abuse so readily. Presumably, since the nurse discontinued the use of valium abruptly, her use of it was probably still rather moderate. Even so, the story illustrates the fact intelligent people, well aware of the dangers of substance abuse, are not beyond its perils when in the wake of post-divorce experience. The nurse knew she was lucky in extricating herself from developing addiction. Others are not so lucky. In talking to many prominent divorcees, I was astonished to learn a physician or airline pilot or some pillar of the community (who everyone thought led a very stable and self-controlled life) was, in fact, an addict and had been for years. When exploring these stories further, one often finds the addictions began when the person first sensed he or she was losing control over his or her life. It is extraordinary how often this occurs shortly before or after a divorce.

Workaholism

In the wake of divorce, some find refuge in work, lots of work… lots and lots and lots of work. For the workaholic, work insulates the individual from reflecting on the difficulties of the past and present. It also distracts the person from the challenges of an active social life. For work to sufficiently protect the person from the intrusions of ordinary life, it must be all consuming. Scott Thurow in his book *One* tells of a man who entered Harvard Law School one year after a difficult divorce. When the student was not studying or talking law he anguished over the failure of his marriage. The all-consuming pace of Harvard Law provided a handy refuge for one who was running from the torturous thought of a failed marriage. To excel at Harvard Law School, there is little time available for anything beyond study and participation in the initiation process producing a Harvard Law graduate. Thus, in this case, as in most cases of post-divorce workaholism, the divorcee was able to find a socially approved strategy for escaping from the challenges of divorce recovery.

Actually, society-at-large often benefits from this escape ploy. I know of more than one scholar who produced his best work during the first few years following a divorce. It is easy to become absorbed in one's research or writing. If one's mind begins to drift, it immediately shows itself in a diminished capacity for writing. Consequently, the newly-disciplined scholar is constantly reminded to stick to the task at hand and produce orderly, informative exposition. Similarly, doctors and lawyers may increase the time they devote to their practices.

Various business-types and engineers may find ways of doing their jobs better or starting a second business. For example, one physicist who worked on a high-tech project for the federal government found he could while away his time alone by creating computer programs aimed at developing psychomotor skills in brain-injured patients. His software design activities became all-consuming and as the months became years, he seemed oblivious to the fact he went from work to his home computer terminal sometimes even forgetting to eat. He was not by nature a recluse.

Prior to the divorce he and his wife pursued a "swinging" lifestyle. For several years after the divorce, he became wedded to his job and software design activities. He was seemingly no longer interested in pursuing relationships with women nor even comradely ones with male pals. His work provided the sanctuary he felt he needed. All in all, society may find the energy of these workaholics much to their liking. The achievements of the workaholic may make the world a more pleasant place for the rest of us. Unfortunately, there is often no such benefit to the workaholic.

The person who suddenly accepts the role of workaholic after the divorce is not engaged in a work of love. Unlike the individual for whom work is a passion, the post-divorce workaholic is using work as a sanctuary from the demands of daily social life. The sanctuary can quickly become a prison. The divorcee may be convinced he is thriving because of his increased work output, but as family practitioners and psychologists are quick to note, the post-divorce workaholic's general physical health tells a different story. Hypertension, adult-onset diabetics, migraine headaches, ulcers, hemorrhoids, and even cancer may be just a few months ahead for the workaholic who retreats from the opportunities of social life.

Divorce threatens the public's and the individual's concepts of friendship, duty and commitment. Divorcees typically find it difficult to trust others of the opposite sex. This is because, among other things, they believe themselves to be victims, objects of abandonment, objects of betrayal by their best friends. In addition, the divorcee often becomes estranged from many of his or her married friends to whom the divorcee's singleness is perceived as a threat to their own frail marriages.

For those who initiate divorce, things are not much better. The divorcee may initiate the divorce because he or she decided the relationship had lost a reciprocal sense of commitment. The divorcee's sense that he or she has lost a best friend, as well perhaps as an assortment of other friends, may be traumatic in itself. If the individual initiated the divorce because he or she had set sights on greener pastures, the person's own failure of duty, friendship, and commitment serves public notice the divorcee cannot always be trusted. Indeed, more generally, it suggests that in the world in which we live, people cannot always trust someone they took to be their best friend. In other words, the divorcee's own selfish trek toward greener pastures may haunt him or her with the idea unwavering trust and commitment between lovers is no longer possible. The divorcee may believe others look upon him or her as a source of distrust. To be found out, as it were, as a betrayer, a person the philosopher Jean Paul Sartre describes as a person of bad faith, is devastating to one's self-image.

Finally, when a person loses confidence in the strength and permanence of friendships, this person tends to retreat from the social world altogether. The comfort of such a retreat is increased by one's belief that the importance and substance of one's work are beyond compare with the frivolities of social interactions. When immersing oneself in work, it is easy to conclude there is no greater calling, hence no time for others, no need to trust, no further loss of friendship, and finally, no obligation to act in the best interest of others. Obsessive work patterns suggest the maxim "No man is an island" can be overcome.

The post-divorce workaholic is not by nature anti-social. The divorcee's self-imposed anti-social behavior weighs heavily on the psyche. What each divorcee wants most, the friendship and esteem of others, is denied the person by his or her own timidity and egocentrism.

Making friends, dating, developing any form of intimacy with others, requires a certain amount of risk-taking. Not everyone can be your friend, is trustworthy, or will like you as much as you like them. But you will never know who can be your friend, your lover or who is really trustworthy until you risk the vulnerabilities attendant upon every attempt at intimacy.

Success at work may bring limited esteem for the product of your work but that does not necessarily translate into esteem for your person. Contrary to the apparent intentions of post-divorce workaholics, friendship and the esteem of others remain central to the workaholic's well-being. The workaholic's efforts sabotage the divorcee's desperate quest for happiness. Personal regard and friendship can only be achieved through interpersonal contact with others. Work must be seen for its own value and not as an escape or for its contributions to the individual's personal and social life.

Reclusiveness

Much of what characterizes reclusiveness has already been discussed. The only thing to add here is divorcees who become reclusive without becoming workaholic risk sliding into serious clinical depression. And if alcohol or drugs are involved, the slide into depression may become more rapid, more irretrievable, and more potentially suicidal.

If the slide into depression stops somewhat short of the most extreme effects, the recluse nevertheless remains little more than an observer of his or her own life. There is no recovery from the minutes, hours and days squandered in self-pity or in daydreaming for something better. Life is meant to be lived, moment by moment.

Promiscuity

Psychologists and sociologists often bring to light secrets about human behavior that amaze and astonish lay persons. Other times their research confirms bits of folk wisdom so widely understood it seems a wonder anybody would investigate the matter. Such is the case in the matter of post-divorce promiscuity.

Earlier in this century, women were thought to be the sole receptacles of sexual morality. Divorced women, by contrast, were often perceived as given to "fits of sin." A woman "needed" a man, it was thought, so when she became widowed, or worse yet, cast off by a man, she found herself in desperate need of male companionship. She was apt to haunt any social affair (even bars!) looking for available men, even a wayward husband. A divorced woman had to be careful her condition of aloneness did not become the subject of malicious gossip.

Many women alone because of divorce *were lonely*, as were many divorced men. What could be more reasonable than to attend social gatherings with the intention, in part, of meeting available people of the opposite sex? Why divorced women and not men were likely to attract so much public condemnation is very much a mystery. The standard feminist retort, "It was a sexist world," will not do, for other women were just as likely, if not more so, than men to cast a suspicious eye toward the activities of a divorced woman.

Sixty-plus years ago, it would have been difficult to determine the frequency with which divorced people engaged in sex. For the most part, all a lay observer could have relied on were the rumors and innuendos of other equally ignorant observers. Who *knows* what goes on behind closed doors? Only the participants knew and sixty-plus years ago, they were not talking.

Things are quite different today. The sixties brought with it the free love movement and a three-fold increase in the divorce rate. Today the pendulum has begun to swing in the other direction. In part, current conventions in sexual behavior and the concomitant decrease in the divorce rates is a predictable reaction to the excesses and superficiality of the sixties and early seventies. AIDS, and, to a lesser extent, herpes and chlamydia (yeast infection) have also made promiscuous sexual behavior less acceptable.

Baby boomers who once led the fight against the sexual mores of earlier generations now see the havoc wreaked on people as a result of broken relationships, broken marriages, and indiscriminate affairs. An unparalleled generation of single parent families now exists. Thousands of children now live with one parent… and someone else, occasionally visiting an estranged parent (and often another family) on weekends and in the summer. Counselor's offices have become home to baby boomers trying to "find themselves" or learn what went awry with what had seemed like such a promising and enlightened life-plan. The baby boomers themselves have become the first to condemn the results. Political polls for the last fifteen years consistently reveal baby boomers are increasingly conservative.

Baby boomers have ascended as a political and social force. They may not be happy with the world they are making, but it truly is a world of their making.

Public reflection on hitherto private sexual matters has become quite common as a result of the sexual revolution. Whenever the ratings for a television talk show decrease, a temporary recovery can be secured by having baby boomers talk about their sexual interests or the inadequacies of their personal relationships. Sex and the nature of intimate relationships is now a topic of general concern.

Most people believe "Nearly everyone goes through a period of promiscuity following a divorce." There probably is no other single proposition so conventionally accepted by divorcees, regardless of personal background.

First, what counts as promiscuity? Second, how does promiscuity begin? Third, are there different forms of promiscuity? Fourth, is promiscuity different for men than for women? Fifth, is promiscuity really such a bad thing? Sixth, if promiscuity should be avoided, how does one reasonably go about doing so?

According to *Webster's Ninth New Collegiate Dictionary,* promiscuity is "a miscellaneous mixture or mingling of persons or things." Only secondarily does it indicate "promiscuous sexual behavior, esp.: Not restricted to one sexual partner." The colloquial use of the term promiscuity among the divorced is inherently tied to sexual intercourse with a multiplicity of partners, and it has a negative connotation. Even today, living as we do on the heels of the sexual revolution, people are generally not flattered when accused of being promiscuous. One may comfortably "fess up" to dating a variety of people but take offense at the suggestion he or she is sleeping with them. Perhaps it was once "cool" to have many sexual partners and to be free in the expression of one's erotic impulses. Things are different now. Current political and social conservatism have made people more restrained in their sexual behavior. More pronounced, however, is the effect of venereal diseases such as AIDS and herpes. One who admits to participation in an active sexual life may find potential partners harder to come by. Sex is less and less a focal point of adult play. Instead, it is increasingly seen as a threat to one's physical well-being. Consequently, people are demanding more of a relationship before they engage in intercourse. They seek commitment from a prospective partner, but just as important they want some assurance the partner has been "careful," selective and, generally, has not played around. People who have been divorced for several years may admit to being promiscuous shortly following their divorce but now feel constrained from much physical contact until after they learn something about an intended partner's sexual past. As one forty-ish computer operator remarked:

> Four years ago when I first got divorced, I haunted the bars looking for a quick one night stand. I don't think there is anything morally wrong with complete sexual freedom—in fact, during the last couple of years of our marriage I tried convincing my wife we might improve our life by engaging in some mate-swapping with other couples. Now, I date one girl just to assure I can have safe sex. Originally, I intended to cheat on her from time to time, but how do you know who it's safe to cheat with? A girl eager to have a one night stand with you has prob-

ably been eager to have one night stands with lots of others.

A lot of my friends are still drifting from partner to partner. They laugh about AIDS but their laughter seems, well... sort of nervous. The topic of condoms is jovially bantered about—but no one talked or even joked about condoms a few years ago.

Since I'm still single, I don't feel I'm committed to the girl I date. But before I even contemplate switching to another, I am going to find out all I can about her past love life before I switch.

This fellow is very much a product of the sexual revolution. One might even go further and condemn him as a male chauvinist who views women as mere tools to be used for his own sexual gratification. By his own account, he is a promiscuous person. It is interesting to note several characteristics of this individual.

First, his early post-divorce sexual exploits were apparently many and indiscriminate. Now he maintains one relationship as the sole release of his sexual energy. Do we want to say he is less promiscuous? When the computer operator's story was related to a number of women, there was general agreement that he was still a *promiscuous person*. They were quick to point out only his fear of AIDS prevented him from continuing with a series of one night stands. More than one woman observed, "As soon as they find a cure or a vaccine for AIDS that guy will drop his girlfriend and be 'hitting the bars again.'" These women regarded promiscuity as being a matter extending beyond the count of his sexual conquests. Promiscuity, from the women's view, fixed on the *intent* of the man to engage in intercourse as often as fortune and safety allow.

Men were more divided in their assessment of the computer operator's current status. Nearly all the men with whom I spoke agreed this fellow did not seem like a nice person. Some argued if he were committed to having sexual intercourse with one and only one partner, then he was not promiscuous. They admitted, however, were it not for the presence of AIDS, he would immediately return to his previous life-style. But as long as he remained loyal to his current girlfriend, then in their opinion he was not promiscuous. The majority of men disagreed, however. They, like all the women, thought the concepts of *commitment* and *loyalty* are key concepts in making a *responsible assessment* of another person's promiscuity. As one salesman noted, "Besides his previous record of one night stands, you said he admitted to looking for a more attractive girl even now. And if he could find one and feel confident she was 'safe,' he'd drop his current girlfriend and move on to the more promising option. That strikes me as promiscuous."

Thus, while it appears the word promiscuous suggests multiple sexual partners, there is another sense of the word that more accurately reflects the interest of most of today's adult singles. This second sense of the term is closely related to *Webster's:* "a miscellaneous mixture or mingling of persons or things." In this sense of the word, there is no *explicit* reference to sexual intercourse. Rather, the concern is with the individual's unwillingness or inability to commit to one other person.

For most people, commitment is a matter of being faithful to one other person. Romantic intercourse, that experience wherein one attempts to explore the recesses of another's soul and, in the process, become vulnerable to the other's efforts to do the same, need not involve the act of copulation. Clearly, one can copulate without feeling romantic, but to engage in romantic intercourse awakens expectations one's partner is compellingly drawn to the contemplation of a blossoming union. Each person hopes the lover finds the other an object of fascination, a person whose mind, body, and heart deserve and require further and intense investigation. With each effort to learn more, the lover becomes more vulnerable to the reciprocal soul-searching advances of the beloved. Romance forces lovers to take risks, to expose themselves in ways they would not in cases of mere friendship or sexual playfulness. Since sexual intercourse is one of the most intimate and personal acts, it is natural for most people to associate sexual intimacy with romance and to seek fulfillment through sexual intercourse. However, romance without sex is certainly a common possibility and a person who seeks sexual intimacy to the exclusion of romance is deliberately precluding further thoughts of commitment.

Professor Roger Scruton aptly remarks through our touches and caresses it is as if we bring the soul of the other person to the surface of the body. Scruton is correct when he goes on to explain this "coming to the surface of the body" is what makes a sexual encounter successful and more pleasant than merely having one's body touched. It is the *thought* of the other person's interest that makes the human sexual experience more than a mere biological event. To settle for the mere biology of it all is, from the perspective of most middle-class people today, to be a promiscuous human being.

Sooner or later most divorced people will enter the social melee of adult singles. To preserve self-esteem during this period, divorcees go through a period in which they attempt to *make* each date a success. For a while—at least for some people—this may well amount to 'making' each date. The sexual aggressiveness of the few does not account for the perception among divorcees themselves that nearly everyone goes through a promiscuous period following divorce. So if most divorcees are not promiscuous persons but fall victim to a transient promiscuous period, what is the nature of this transitioning experience?

Presumably, the promiscuity during this "passage" is of an explicitly sexual sort, but surely, for most it is free of the vicious egocentrism of the promiscuous person.

A Theory of Flirtation

Everyone has heard the expression an "innocent flirtation." Such flirtations are fun and tend to *relieve* the tension in a potentially strained social affair. Innocent flirtations are almost exclusively verbal. They bring comic relief and warmth to social events too serious or too boring. Characteristic features of an innocent flirtation include the following: it is highly verbal and the voice of the flirt invariably rings with good cheer. Second, an innocent flirtation is typically addressed toward someone whose looks, position in life, and so on make it all but impossible to mistake the flirtation for something more intense. Third, there are no longing gazes, blushing glances, or touches to sensitive areas of the other's body. Fourth, an innocent flirtation involves no sense of sexual excitement but instead produces the same fun feeling as telling or listening to a good joke. While it is difficult to give an example of different kinds of flirtation in print, people universally agree important differences exist. And most people believe they can spot a flirtation for what it is.

Nearly every divorcee will become flirtatious for a time. Singles flirt to gain a sense of the opposite sex's responsiveness. When re-entering the single world, every divorcee hopes his or her presence will be well-received. For most, there is a fear one's availability will go unnoticed. Consequently, when venturing into the single's scene, people attempt to tantalize their opposites. This means engaging in some sort of flirtation.

Is flirtatious behavior bad? Not always, perhaps not even generally. Even so, each trip to the bedroom begins with some act of flirtation. One must consider, then, when a propensity to flirt goes beyond the engagement of another's attention and towards a more general predisposition to be promiscuous.

To avoid promiscuous behavior, must one avoid flirting? Is flirting itself a form of promiscuity? Happily, the answer to both these questions is a resounding "No!" because flirting is a time-honored tradition in the world of romance. It is an effective way to show a special interest in others. Flirting is a practice as natural and appropriate in the dating scene as hand-holding, kissing, and all the rest. But people recognize different types of flirtation and different types of flirtatious people. Some are objectionable and some are not.

My point in describing promiscuity, the theory of flirtation, and the judgmental habits of others is to alert the reader to events and behaviors inhibiting the search for intimacy. To be promiscuous destroys one's options for intimacy. Even to *appear* promiscuous is problematic for those interested in establishing enduring relationships with others. All moral judgments aside, it is in the divorcees' best social interest to avoid sexually solicitous flirtations or any other behavior leading to condemnation for promiscuous activity.

My theory of flirtation is meant to serve as a guide to "experienced amateurs"—middle-aged adults hitting the single's scene for the first time in a long time—so they may avoid the pitfalls of appearing promiscuous and succeed in engaging the respectful attention of others. While there are many clear-cut instances of innocent, serious, and sexually solicitous flirtations, there are also many instances of hybrid combinations. The hybrids are the consequence of two factors.

First, sometimes it is the actor's intention to inflate an initially innocent flirtation into a more serious one or increase the potency of a serious flirtation but still avoid the consequences of sexually solicitous flirtations. Second, although divorcees may have intuited the distinctions among different types of flirtation in their youth, years of married life make it difficult at first to recover their skills in these matters. Consequently, flirtations intended to be serious are clumsily acted out in a way that makes them *look* innocent, sexually solicitous, or sometimes just nondescript. In the first case, the flirt's designs on another are frustratingly deemed a piece of humor. In the second, one is believed to be on the make. And in the third, one's intentions may go unnoticed altogether.

Trying to recapture one's skills in flirtation requires practice. Divorcees are advised to err in favor of a too-subdued serious or innocent flirtation rather than in the more inflammatory direction of the sexually solicitous flirtation. It is a lot easier—and safer—to go unnoticed a few times rather than get noticed in the wrong way.

The reader will recognize the sense in which the following examples exhibit different types of flirtation.

Imagine if you will, the current Miss America visiting her church. The preacher is five feet two inches tall and weighs generously over two hundred pounds. He comments Miss America looks lovely and always has. He goes on to say she must have every boy in town fawning over her. Miss America reaches for his arm, smiling at his wife, and then at him, saying, "You sweet-talking man, if you weren't married to this lovely lady, I'd cast them all aside for one date with you." All comfortably chuckle at this exchange, enjoying the pleasant and jovial atmosphere it creates.

Then there is the real thing: the serious flirtation which is also an invitation. It says to the person to whom it is directed, "I find you interesting and I invite you to learn more about me." Of course, one may be timid, or suspect the game is better played by indirectly negotiating for position. One may seek acknowledgement of one's intentions before committing to more overt action. This is the purpose of a serious flirtation.

Several features distinguish the serious from the innocent flirtation. First, serious flirtations are less verbal. Verbal cues are limited and, what few exist, aim at getting the other to talk more about him or herself. The goal is to show the flirt finds the other especially interesting. "What's it like to be a pilot?" or "I've always thought models have such great poise" are examples of this sort of maneuver. Second, a serious flirtation is directed at someone who could conceivably take a reciprocal interest in the flirt. Third, the flirt's body language expresses unmitigated attention to the other's actions: leaning forward to listen intently, smiling warmly and through the eyes showing that one is wholly absorbed in the other's talk. Fourth, one is quite conscious of the other as a sexual being. There is a *hint of sexual excitement*. More important, there is the evident desire to learn more about the other *as a person*.

Imagine a formal dinner with a dozen or so people. Instead of joining in the general banter, the serious flirt expresses interest in a targeted person by showing he or she is wholly absorbed in all the other says and does. The flirt's actions show, whatever else is going on, there is little else of any immediate interest. For example, the flirt makes every effort to position him or herself in order to keep an optimal amount of eye contact while barely avoiding a sexually-solicitous stare.

A third type of flirtation is the sexually solicitous flirtation. This highly volatile ploy invites the other to consider the flirt as an immediately available sexual object. Coming right out and asking someone for a date is hardly flirtatious. It is a way of laying one's cards on the table. First, the most pronounced feature of the sexually solicitous flirtation is the use of the eyes. In such flirtations what is said is usually inconsequential. Rather, it is the steady gaze of the eyes which signal to the other, "I am alertly aware of you as a sexual object."

Second, like the serious flirtation, this act is usually directed toward someone the flirt hopes will respond. Third, the body language becomes ever more inviting. No longer showing mere interest such as directing one's face and body toward the other, the solicitous sexual flirtation involves expansive body gestures on the part of the male and shoe dangling or leg-crossing on the part of the female. More important, there may be acts of touching. For example, if a flirt shakes the hand of another, he or she will intently hold the hand longer than ordinary social decorum would prescribe. The male may move his body closer to the female and even put his arm around her, holding more steadily and tightly than one might with a mere friend. The female may touch the front of the man's trunk and maneuver herself more closely to his side, lightly allowing her hips or breasts to touch his legs or arms, respectively. A sexually solicitous flirt is likely to place her hand on the leg of the other when the occasion presents itself. Some parts of a person's body may be touched by others without objection, but clearly other parts are off limits. Sexually solicitous flirtation is daring in its refusal to respect these boundaries. Fourth, one intends the other to notice him or her *as a sexually responsive creature*, to prompt the other into some obvious act of recognition. Fifth, this volatile form of flirtation is the one most likely to lead to a sexual encounter. Consequently, it is not surprising others regard this last form of flirtation as conclusive evidence of promiscuity.

Innocent flirtations never lead to promiscuity. Serious flirtations are generally not a source of promiscuous behavior nor suggestive of promiscuous intentions. Sexually solicitous flirtations often result in casual sex. More important, they are nearly always perceived as evidence of a promiscuous personality.

The danger of engaging in sexually solicitous flirtation is three-fold. First, it leads observers to view the flirt as a promiscuous personality. Second, it causes the person flirted with to view the flirt as a sexual object only. If the flirt is hoping for a more serious commitment, this technique is a misfire. Third, since this flirtation is perceived as an invitation to engage in sexual activity, the flirt may soon find himself or herself caught up in an unintended scene which he or she genuinely wishes to avoid.

The existence of the promiscuous personality has long been recognized as a standard category in both our folk wisdom and in the psychological and psychiatric literature. Unfortunately, its description is not well articulated in folk wisdom and fares little better in the professional literature. For example, a female with a promiscuous personality is likely to be identified as a nymphomaniac. In the professional literature, nymphomania is defined as " excessive sexual desire by a female." Ordinary folks, both men and women alike, less delicately describe a "nympho" as one who likes to "hump" a lot. Men who are regarded as promiscuous types are thought to be indiscrete, careless, and thoughtless about the bodies they press to their own. While in an earlier, more chauvinistic era, some may have idolized the Don Juan who was able to woo numerous attractive lovers, things have changed. While the Don Juan is still contrasted with the pathetic male who indiscriminately seeks any opportunity for copulation, neither is an object of admiration. Being identified as a promiscuous type is no longer a compliment even for the immature male.

Finally, research into incest has discovered one of the most predictable out-runners of an incestuous childhood is adult promiscuity (often followed by periods of frigidity under conditions of genuine intimacy.) As this information becomes more accessible, men and women may have yet another reason to fear the appearance of promiscuity since it may suggest a lot more about a person's past than the person may care to divulge. And, finally, as E. Susan Blume explains in her in-depth book *Secret Survivor: Uncovering Incest and its After Effects in Women,* both sexes, but particularly women, ought to consider the possibility their promiscuous habits may well be symptomatic of childhood incest, in which case professional help should be sought.

Judgments of another's promiscuity are not based solely on the frequency or variety of one's affairs. It is the *perception* of what the person is up to that attracts the name. A person is regarded as promiscuous based on public behavior and not on actual bedroom escapades! Since no reasonable person enjoys public condemnation (the innocent and heroic Hester Prynne of Nathaniel Hawthorne's *Scarlet Letter* did not enjoy her status as a "dishonored" woman), no one would set out to incur the rebuke of peers. Still, there are men and women who so regularly engage in the practice of sexually solicitous flirtation they all but force their friends and associates to regard them as promiscuous. If this is an unreasonable thing to do, and if these people seem generally reasonable in most other areas of their lives, what could account for such irrational behavior? To understand such persistent irrationality, one must understand the nature of addiction.

People are addicted to a substance or practice when *against all reason* they act to ingest dangerous substance or engage in self-destructive behavior. For example, the alcoholic may function for years as a successful business person or congressional representative, but the alcoholic persistently drinks too much knowing well the erosion to health, as well as social and professional success. Psychologists, as well as many alcoholics themselves, report the individual's insecurity feeds addictive patterns of behavior. The alcoholic, for example, drinks to feel a quick elation or to forget past wrongs and inadequacies. The more pressure alcoholics feel, the more likely they are to drink.

The promiscuous personality, too, is driven by fears, insecure about who they are, about what they have done right as well as wrong. The most expeditious way for getting re-affirmation of their merit is to solicit the attention of others by appealing to their most base sexual instincts. It takes a while to get others to evaluate and applaud one's ideas, talents or moral worth. Sexually solicitous flirtations produce much more immediate and visible results. Insecure people need approval of their worth. Unfortunately for the flirt, what comes easily on the surface—others' favorable attention—may bring disrespect in the long run. People sometimes give public approval to behaviors they privately despise. Flirts, as well as anyone else seeking approval, want genuine regard from others and not just the appearance of such.

The insecure person never learned to delight in his or her own personal or professional achievements. Sexual affirmation becomes their addictive substitute. People are quick to respond to a sexual advance, so flirts think they are getting rewarded when their solicitations succeed. An affirmative response to the flirt's sexual advance is direct, personal and sincere—the other sincerely accepts the flirt's implied invitation. But acceptance of such an invitation does not carry with it respect or admiration. And the desire for those drive the insecure flirt in the first place.

Promiscuous personalities are often successful in many areas of life, having acquired many public and visible achievements, but their own irrational doubt leads them to seek the quick fix: instant gratification of their desire to be valued. Just as the alcoholic cannot believe in his or her own merit but instead grasps for the distraction of the bottle, promiscuous personalities also seek distraction from their own self-doubts.

Often the promiscuous personality has resplendent resources with which they can appeal to members of the opposite sex. Consequently, one might expect the flirt's confidence in this area would be so strong he or she would need no reassurance. In actual practice, the situation of the promiscuous personality seems to be analogous to the accumulation of great wealth. When people are economically secure and comfortable, they are prone to be charitable in time, money, and effort toward others. When they accumulate great wealth, as Aristotle long ago observed, they become greedy and increasingly unhappy. The accuracy of Aristotle's prediction can be borne out by reading in the daily paper the criminal business practices of the already very rich. It is not necessarily a shortage of resources leading one to seek immediate approval of his or her worth. It is simply the person's conviction he or she is not... should not... cannot... be worth much.

The quick fix of the sexual response helps mask one's fears that if people really knew him or her, they would find the person unattractive, perhaps even reprehensive. The more insecure the promiscuous personality feels, the more frequently the person engages in sexually solicitous flirtations. The most classic example of this, the well-heeled older man with a proclivity for dating many younger women. He may be with the most beautiful woman in a restaurant or at a social affair, yet he feels compelled to gaze into the eyes of the waitress or some other woman, all but ignoring his date. He may repeatedly survey the surroundings, looking for any reasonably attractive woman willing to return his steady, solicitous gaze.

In discussing this classic example with three attractive women, each a graduate student in psychology, the conversation which followed was illuminating. First, upon hearing the scenario, all immediately burst into laughter saying, "I've been out with him." One, a raven-haired former model said, "They don't have to be old, either, though they do seem to get worse as they get older." A pert and baby-faced blonde in her late twenties observed:

I have only been out with one guy like that, and I should have seen it coming. I was working in a very exclusive shoe emporium when this guy, about forty or so, comes in with a girl my age. He bought her three pairs of expensive shoes. I couldn't figure out if she was his daughter or not. She was much younger than he, but she didn't seem young enough to be his daughter. The whole time she was trying on shoes, I could feel him staring at me. I was flattered but, at the same time, I was nervous.

If they were a couple, she might notice his stares and want to leave without buying anything. When he paid for the shoes, he seemed to be showing off for my benefit as much as hers. It was strange.

About three days later, he called me at work and asked if I would join him for lunch, and I did. At lunch, he asked me out for the next evening. I agreed. Anytime we were alone he was polite, very pleasant—he was almost shy!

When we were at the restaurant, he did that staring thing. It embarrassed me. It made me feel like chopped liver. I felt like everyone around knew I was just being taken advantage of, some little bimbo, and that he was on the make.

On the way home, he again became very nice and even gentlemanly. He was flirtatious as we moved toward the door, but there was no way I was going to invite him in—even if he were the head of his own company and "friends" with all sorts of important people. When we were in public, he made me feel like I was a loser and could be bought. When we were alone, he made me feel that I should be impressed with his importance and the fact that he seemed overwhelmed by my beauty or whatever.

Throughout this girl's anecdote the other two periodically chimed in with vigorous agreement, excitedly declaring, "That's true! That's just the way those guys are!" The girl who related the story said the man called her three or four times afterwards seeking another date despite her obvious coolness toward him.

The third woman, a statuesque thirty-one-year old, added, (again to the agreement of the other two):

> Those kind of guys are so weird. They always act like you mean so much to them. But as soon as you are nice to them or they get in a crowd, they act as if the most important thing in the world is to flirt and get attention from someone—anyone—else! They always seem to be signaling, "Hey, I'm available baby and I could show you a really good time... know what I mean, honey."

When asked if there were women like this, they agreed there were. The characteristic example was of a coquettish high school or college girl. The former model observed:

> She's the one at the parties who's always looking to turn someone on—usually someone else's boyfriend. Just like the old guy, it doesn't make any difference who she is with, she is always looking to make some other guy crazy. She can even be with her boyfriend, but anytime he isn't paying particularly close attention to her, she has usually picked out one other guy that she keeps gazing at. When the other guy returns

her stare, she often acts like she's embarrassed, looks away and then shortly begins looking back at him. The funny thing is the guy seems to get the impression that he's just irresistible to her when, in fact, she's just entertaining herself.

The other two laughed in agreement. One of the three related the following story:

> There was a girl in our high school who seemed to have everything, good grades, great looks, money. Her parents were divorced so she would also have periods of considerable freedom when she was visiting her Dad. Her mother was much stricter. She was a part of our group, you know, one of our friends, supposedly.
>
> But since she seemed so hell-bent on getting every boy who was halfway cute to make a play for her, it always seemed to us she was just waiting to snatch away our dates. She never seemed to go with boys long. Either the boy would drop her because he wouldn't put up with her flirting or, as soon as it was clear she had the boy, she would drop him.
>
> We all thought she was a shameless hussy, doing it with nearly every guy she went out with. Certainly, the guys looked forward to having a date with her! But to be honest it was never really clear if she was doing any more than petting with them. When the rest of us started having our first sexual experiences, sometime around our junior year, she always insisted she was a virgin. So who knows?

> She married some guy she met her sophomore year in college. They got divorced when she went to law school. Now she's married again to the guy who used to be her boss but that marriage is supposed to be in trouble, too. She's supposedly having an affair with another lawyer. She'll probably never settle down, [because] married or not she just seems, as you say, to be perpetually promiscuous.

I asked why they thought of an older man when asked about a classic example of a sexually promiscuous male and a young woman when they thought of examples of a sexually promiscuous female. Although puzzled at first, they all agreed there can be sexually promiscuous males and females at any age but there is a tendency to make a sex/age distinction when thinking of the most typical examples. One speculated, "Maybe there is just no one for the older woman to flirt with. The guys just keep dying off and the ones that are left keep looking for younger girls." Another speculated, "I don't agree. I think maybe women are just better at realizing that transitory relationships aren't worth much. If you can't get a real, lasting commitment in a relationship then it's just not worth much. It's better to be alone than spending all your time playing silly games." The third woman, tentatively agreeing with the second added, "Women friends are important to women. If a woman keeps up a promiscuous image, she starts losing all her girlfriends."

If the sexually promiscuous personality is so costly to its owner, why do some men and women persistently manifest such behavior? The answer is twofold. First, the personality trait is addictive. Without appropriate counseling, the trait remains a defining feature of one's self-concept. Second, the trait is sufficiently reinforced in society to ensure its continuation. For example, the promiscuous personality is a commonly portrayed stereotype in movies, television, and our culture. Have we not made a hero out of Magic Johnson? In addition, as the student who sold shoes noted, "There is something flattering, at first, about being the object of so much explicit sexual attention by someone who really does seem... well, you know, together." Much later in my meeting with the three graduate students, the model said something very revealing:

> I've gotten hooked up with three of those guys so far. I was starting to worry if there was something wrong with me—maybe there is! Ha, ha. But you're right. Some of those people really do have something going for them until you discover they're such shallow people and losers at intimacy.

Men's impressions of the promiscuous personality differ little from women's. The sexually indiscriminate male is often described by his peers as a loser while the sexually-active, but selective, Don Juan is written off as an "ass." Men agree with women on the classic examples of the male and female manifestations of the promiscuous personality. When asked why the classic examples reflected a sex/age distinction, one physician observed, "I think women just learn that having a promiscuous personality is a real turn off to any man looking for a relationship. Men, on the other hand, never seem to learn—until," he added, smiling, "we get too old to do anything about it."

The "promiscuous personality" is a deeply imbedded category in our folk psychology. To be labeled as such becomes a real detriment to one seeking a serious relationship and to one's social life in general. People quickly lose interest in inviting a man or woman to a party if that person's presence will have a disruptive effect on the affair.

A second danger in the use of sexually solicitous flirtations is it causes the object of the flirtation to lose sight of you *as a person*. In a sexually solicitous flirtation, you invite people to see you *as a sex object* and not as a person. Consequently, if the flirtation is successful and the other responds, he or she is looking to you as a potential sex partner and any effort on your part to show different aspects of your personality will be regarded as a mere distraction. If you persist in trying to redirect the focus of the other, you may find yourself regarded as fickle, immature, or a tease. In any case, you will find you have got the relationship off to a bad start if not blown it all together.

One thirty-year-old engineer explained her experiences:

> I was pretty chunky by the time I got divorced. So after I got over feeling sorry for myself, I started dieting and joined an exercise class. I started looking good. I went down two dress sizes to an eight! At different times, I agreed to be fixed up by my friends, to go out with men from work, one man from my exercise class and two or three guys I met at night clubs. I was so eager that they each see me as attractive.
>
> I worked on my "sultry" looks, my walk, my car-exiting behavior and so on. I really wanted these guys to be turned on by me—and, except for one, they were. The trouble was they didn't know or care about me. They just wanted my body. I started thinking all men were boors. Still, I kept trying harder and harder to be an irresistible siren. I figured I was getting men with what I was doing. I was just going to have to persist until the right one came along.

Finally, something very important happened. Susan, my best friend during most of my marriage, joined me for lunch one day. Our relationship had become a bit strained since the divorce. It hurt my feelings, but I knew that people often lost their married friends once they became divorced. During our lunch, I made several rather pointed remarks indicating that I felt abandoned by Susan and several other of my married friends.

Eventually, Susan took the bull by the horns and responded, "You've changed." She went on to say that she and the others had supported me after the divorce, but after I lost weight and started dressing racier my behavior changed as well. She said that she and the other women felt I was flirting with their husbands. I couldn't believe it. Not only had I never intended to flirt with any of their husbands but I retaliated to her suggestion by saying "Maybe you all are just threatened by having a single women in your midst."

I was about to go on and tell her that married women tend to let themselves go to pot, as I had, and if we did more to keep ourselves attractive, we wouldn't be so easily threatened by a divorcee. Before I had a chance to, Susan started pointing out things I had done. She was right. Without even thinking about it, I had started trying out my new "skills" such as sitting next to a man on a couch, slightly angled, knees touching, hand on his leg and looking tentatively (she said) into his eyes while he told me about his kid's little league adventures.

The more she said, the more I discovered she was right. I also remembered that I thought a couple of the husbands were real Bozos the way they kept coming on to me. Maybe there was something I was doing. Maybe that's why my dates and other men I met seemed reluctant to want to learn about me.

I started watching myself and trying to unlearn some of the things I worked so hard to develop. It was difficult at first, but I managed. What really amazed me was that I no longer had to work so hard to get guys. I learned that I was attractive enough that men would make a point of meeting me. It was all casual, friendly and fun. If you decide you like a man, you can let him know it without all that sex stuff. I'm glad I learned my sex skills because now after I've been dating someone for quite some time, I can let him know through my actions it is time for some intimacy. But this is all done away from the prying eyes of others. In these special and very private cases with someone special, sexual flirtations are fun and in good taste, I think.

Remember, flirtations are an invitation. The innocent flirtation invites another to share in a joke, a bit of merrymaking. The serious flirtation invites the other to learn more about you. The sexually solicitous flirtation invites the other to know only your body. When extending invitations, know who you are inviting and to what sort of affair.

The third reason you should avoid the sexually solicitous flirtations is they can provoke some very awkward encounters. As one forty-two-year old woman related:

I was at a night club with some of my friends. There was this gorgeous-looking man whom I guessed to be about three years younger than I. I had only been out on a couple of dates since my divorce two years ago, and I was lonely. And, I guess, I was horny, too. I kept staring at the guy until I caught his eye. Then for the next fifteen minutes we flirted with our eyes until finally he walked up and asked me to dance. The first dance was fast, and I tried to wiggle everything that was supposed to wiggle. I didn't even worry that other parts that weren't supposed to jiggle, jiggled. If he was going to notice my worst parts as well as my best, I'd have no chance anyway. He seemed entertained, and I was sure having a good time as well. Later we did a slow dance. He pulled me very close to him. I responded by moving my hands inside his suit coat, slowly moving them around to his back.

We talked and he offered to drive me the three blocks to my home. We parked outside my apartment for a few minutes, and I was trying to decide whether or not to invite him in. We started kissing; then in a couple of minutes, he was just out and out groping me. I tried to slow him down, but he just got angry. It all turned ugly, fast. My blouse got ripped and I don't know what would have happened if I hadn't gotten out and run right to my door.

Sometimes you get more than you bargain for. I mean, he seemed like a real decent sort at first. What do you suppose makes a guy like that act like such a jerk. I'm staying out of bars even if it means I don't get any dates except with an occasional friend from work or my church group.

Being inexperienced in the ways of the single's scene can lead an unsuspecting person to send out the wrong message. In addition, since sexually solicitous flirtations have the potential for inducing intense behavior on the part of others, know who you are flirting with lest you imperil yourself.

A thirty-three-year old school teacher with a kind face and gentle voice explained that men, too, can find themselves embarrassed by careless or inappropriate flirtations:

> I got a date with this nurse through my online dating club. Her face was okay and the rest of her was dynamite. We went out, got a pizza, chatted and then things started getting steamy. I don't know how it happened or who started it. Suddenly, we were looking directly into each other's eyes, and I just knew that I was going to go to bed with her. Driving back to her place, she sat very close to me and put her hand on my leg. I was going crazy!
>
> When we got to her place, we kissed in front of her apartment. It seemed as though there was no part of the front of her body that wasn't touching mine. She invited me in. I hesitated. I thought, "If I go in, we'll wind up in bed." I also thought, "I hardly know this girl. Hell, if she's this easy with me she's got to be this way with lots of other guys." That alone would have bothered me ten years ago... but I would have probably gone through with it. Now, with AIDS ever present, the whole situation gets scarier.
>
> Anyway, I went in thinking I would find out how far she was willing to go. But, because of the AIDS thing, I wouldn't go through with it. Things began

cooking right away. We took my shirt off and then we took all her clothes off. She wanted to do the whole thing. I declined. Then she said she would be happy if she could show me a few things with her mouth. Again, because of the AIDS thing, I declined and said I really had to be going. I couldn't believe I was turning down this opportunity! But I was worried—things had gone just a little too fast for my tastes.

The thing that really surprised me was that she got mad, real mad! After begging me to stay, she started calling me names and kicked me out of her apartment. She said, "Who do you think you are, playing with people like this?" Maybe she had a point. I don't know. Anyway, I went home wrestling with all sorts of weird feelings. I felt stupid I didn't take advantage of the opportunity. On the other hand, I thought I might be lucky. I thought of the avenging angel with AIDS from the book *The Band Played On*. I also felt maybe I had taken advantage of her feelings. Mostly, I didn't know what to think; I just didn't want anything like that to happen again.

As the teacher points out, it really did not matter how things got started, before long they were out of hand. If the nurse flirted with him in a sexually solicitous manner, she would not have sustained it if he were not responsive, and he may have initiated the flirtation without understanding what he was doing. She may have merely been reciprocating his lead.

A number of psychological studies show some people seem victim prone: some to accidents, some to crime and some to disease. In other words, a certain personality or array of behaviors tends to invite, as it were, the intrusive acts of, say, a careless driver, a criminal, or a disease. Boys going through puberty are often amazed some of their peers, regardless of size or athletic powers, are never bullied or goaded into fighting. Similarly, pubescent girls may wonder why a peer, gorgeous beyond belief, is never the object of the boys' sexist humor. In short, it is often a person's manifest personality which invites trouble and not mere chance.

If people are reacting to you inappropriately in the sexual/social domain review carefully what you are *doing*—NOT just your expressed intentions. When inappropriate behaviors are eliminated from your repertoire of social gestures, people will begin responding to you differently. People enjoy being in control of their destiny. Flirtation of all sorts are ways people attempt to affect others around them. The serious flirtation prompts others to continue in thought-provoking dialogue. In contrast, an accidental but sexually solicitous flirtation frustrates dialogue and may cause the perpetrator to lose control over a situation.

Genuinely promiscuous people seem, one way or another, to be preoccupied with control; they use sexual activity to exercise control over others. A few use sex to submit to others' control and, they hope, their protection as well.

Ralph, a general foreman at a large industrial plant in the upper midwest, was the first to alert me to this phenomenon through a description of his own escapades. The fellow is tall, maybe six foot three. He has dark thick hair which is only now graying at the temples. He was fifty-one-years old when we spoke and in fairly good shape (although the redness of his nose and the spider veins in his cheeks indicated he may have "partied" too much and for too long over the years). His voice is deeply resonant, and he speaks with the confidence of a man who is accustomed to having others carry out his commands. He boasted he had many sexual encounters since his divorce nine years ago but "never with a 'dog.'" He went on to explain he was the kind of guy who just couldn't be happy with one woman. He should have learned that, he said, "... after his first divorce!" But now, three marriages later he is a resolute bachelor and enjoys the control he has over his life and the women in it:

> Sex is fine with a woman until you marry her, then it becomes a weapon for control. As long as they haven't got you, the sex is always available. As soon as you say "I do," they say "not unless you do this, this and this for me first." As long as you stay single, you can have anything you want—including a fair amount of variety.

Control is a major issue here. Commitment to one other person necessarily involves a possible loss of control. To give up control, to act in concert with another, is always risky business and for some, it's too risky. People like Ralph see the risks attendant to commitment as symptomatic of "co-dependency." (One of the more fashionable psychological pathologies making the rounds of self-help literature.) The women in this man's life are to him, like his employees, people to be directed by his command. This man works, plays and co-operates with no one. He controls all he can, submitting only to the non-negotiable demands of his supervisor. When asked if he ever came across a woman of like sentiments, Ralph responded:

I suppose I have, but it would have been inconsequential. We just couldn't get along. Yes, I did. She was a real B—— too, a lady lawyer. She thought my job was to become her lackey. We even argued over who should be on top during sex. As it turns out, we never got around to doing it. I admit it, I'm a monster. I have got to be the boss. I couldn't stand a woman like me anymore than she could stand a man like me!

Ralph fancied himself a modern-day Don Juan. He wanted sexual contact, but he did not want the responsibility attending intimacy. Smiling, he acknowledged he was a flirt. "Yeah, it's one way I get a chuckle at times." More important was his admission control is at the center of his addiction. "You know it's not until you get older that you begin realizing how easy it is to be in the driver's seat with women. And I like that. That's where I was meant to be."

Seeking control through sexual activity is not a male-only addiction. Females, too, can be equally aggressive, seeking control over male counterparts. Consider the story of a thirty-ish television producer with an angelic face, an hour glass figure, and an impeccable taste in clothes. She freely admits to living a promiscuous lifestyle prior to the general spread of AIDS. "Sure, a couple of years ago, during the age of free love, I had a lot of partners. Would I count that as promiscuous? I guess. But wasn't everyone like that in those days?" I asked her if she felt used by the men who made love to her. She responded, "Ah, come on, everybody uses everybody. That's a silly question. This is the real world we are talking about. They wanted me as much as I wanted them so in answer to your question, no, I don't think so." Finally, I asked if she felt she was being manipulated or controlled by some of the men. To that, she coyly smiled and replied:

> You men never know who is in control and who is being controlled. We go home with you or invite you up to our apartment. We send you a signal and you make an advance. And then, if we say something to you like "Take me!" you work yourselves into a frenzy for what, to do our bidding.

She concluded by impishly teasing, "You guys think it's your animal appeal or machismo that drives away our inhibitions. What a joke! Throughout it all we're calling the shots and you're just following our lead."

Contrary to this woman's suggestion, the free-love movement did not lead to universal promiscuity. Her promiscuity, like that of the aging foreman, is reflective of her addictive and controlling personality, her need for control over others and a form of exploitation. They use people to satisfy their own ends. It may well be a comment on our times when some of these users, self-proclaimed sex addicts, solicit freedom from prosecution or public sympathy for excesses by declaring themselves to be victims. (Does anyone really feel sympathy for the author of *Exposing Myself*?) Even victims of incest, who often do exhibit just this sort of promiscuity as well as the second type described below, find few sympathizers in a population generally uninformed about their tragic past and the dim prospects they have for a stable and secure future.

The other side of the control-seeking sexually promiscuous personality is the people who have such low self-esteem they fear the only way they can get others to look after and protect them is to submit to them sexually. This is the personality most commonly portrayed in cheap erotic novels and X-rated movies. While teenage boys are reportedly ever on the alert to finding such girls, and while prostitutes tell stories of masochistic johns, it is not at all clear this is a common personality-profile in the adult world of middle-class America.

No doubt there are some promiscuous types who seek security through being controlled sexually by others. More commonly, it is the promiscuous personality who seeks security through controlling others. In either case, no one's public image is enhanced by being described or thought of as promiscuous as baseball great Wade Boggs, talk-show host Geraldo Rivera, and the Florida policeman's wife (What was her name? How soon we forget!) have discovered. To become the subject of public ridicule is no way to line up future suitors.

Promiscuity is generally thought to be a bad thing. The parallels between the persistently promiscuous and the victim of incest are more than metaphorical. In both cases, the individual is generally not able to enter into the kind of balanced relationship most adults seek. Hence, nearly all people who appear promiscuous are likely to find for one reason or another, few others see them as a good catch.

It may be worthwhile to consider two final examples. First, a group of female co-workers discussing the habit of their boss in a high-tech, space-related industry observed: "He's a great guy. He is kind, nice-looking, dedicated and 'forever a sucker.'" As his former secretary explained:

> He's on wife number four now. They call each other several times each day. He bought her a Mercedes and whatever else she wants. He's constantly spending money on her, and she just keeps asking. It is as if he believes he can only hold on to her if he keeps spending money on

her. Sounds like the latest marriage of a famous Hollywood actress, doesn't it?

> His other wives also call him and ask for money, and he sends it to them! It's as if he's always asking for forgiveness or approval or something. Just before each of the last two marriages he was courting and hopping in and out of bed with every eligible girl around. It was amazing; he couldn't seem to hold on to one. He had all the right sort of equipment. But he is always projecting an image that says, "I'm not good enough, am I?" Boy, it's such a waste. I love to work for him, and I'd like to have him buy me stuff, too, but there's no way I'd ever want to get stuck with a guy like that. It's like he's begging for acceptance every moment.

The second example comes from several middle-aged executives discussing the plight of their friend, a man they feared was about to marry a thirty-two-year old woman who was gorgeous and personable. So what's the problem? What do they fear for their friend? As one quipped:

> He's got to be crazy marrying her. She's banged nearly everyone in the office, and she was that way when she was married to her other husbands. Hey, it's one thing to enjoy a girl like that in bed. But it's just insane to marry her. In two years, she will be up to her old tricks, and in three they will be divorced.

The message the executives gave: it's dangerous to form a relationship with a promiscuous person. Regardless of the detractor's motives (perhaps they were more than just a little jealous?), it is unlikely the woman would have been flattered by their remarks. The moral of the story is, rightly or wrongly, being judged promiscuous is unflattering and detrimental to a successful social life.

Explicit public judgments of promiscuity sound harshly moralistic to the modern ear. Long ago, American author Nathaniel Hawthorne denounced the hypocrisy of branding people who were supposed to have had a single adulterous affair. Why elevate their actions to "sin," normally reserved for acts of violence? And have not the Phil Donahues of "talk and talk" TV gone to great lengths to persuade their audiences of the similar hypocrisy in condemning political candidates for their private indiscretions? Yet in the *real world* of neighborhoods, in which adult singles live, it is ordinarily catastrophic to be labeled by friends and associates as promiscuous.

As one nice woman lamented:

> About six months after my divorce I was invited to a barbecue by friends. There were a few married couples, but mostly it was singles getting a chance to socialize away from the bar scene. I was dressed to kill and did my best to attract the attention of a couple of the bachelors. I never got invited back to any of this group's affairs. One day I asked my friend why no one from the group ever called on me. She said, "Well, you just seemed to throw yourself at everyone. Even the guys thought you were on the make. These are just supposed to be casual affairs that we have. No one really tries to put the make on anyone else. I know that wasn't your intention, but that is the way everyone took it."
>
> I was mortified. I thought I knew what I was doing. I hadn't been drinking. I was just being friendly and trying to let two guys—just two guys—know I was available and interested in them. I spent quite a bit of time with each of the guys in-

dividually. They seemed to like me and like what I was doing. I was being flirtatious, but what else are you supposed to do to let a guy know you're interested? I sat on one guy's lap for a few minutes and that may have been over-doing. No one else had done anything like that, but I figured, "What the heck, nothing ventured, nothing gained." Anyway, I thought the whole thing was innocent enough. I just didn't understand it at the time. Later, as I thought about it, I think maybe I was overzealous. I still don't know quite how... but I know inside I did have the burners turned up to *sizzle*. I mean, who likes to be a wallflower, right? Anyway, I thought I was being quite discreet with my actions. For the most part, I just tried to let my eyes do the talking.

Ah, the eyes. The most inflammatory weapon in the arsenal of the sexually solicitous flirtation. Psychologists and body language experts are just now flushing out the details of how much information is conveyed by the eyes. Ordinary folks, however, with no theory at all, have long recognized when it comes to conveying information of an interpersonal nature, particularly of a sexual sort, the eyes have it. Unlike the other two types of flirtations, words are unimportant, the eyes dominate and set the stage for all else that follows. To avoid unintended sexually solicitous flirtation, pay particular attention to the use of your eyes. Not far behind the eyes in importance is characteristic body language and touching the body of another. Touches can signal a bond of friendship and respect as quickly as fiery sexual interest. It is imperative these signals be unambiguous so one can avoid conveying the wrong impression.

One graying, divorced, military officer in his late thirties, George, was guilty of the two actions above, and, as a result, had to learn some lessons the hard way. He related the following embarrassing account:

I met a girl at a party. We kept looking at each other. I know she was attracted to me. I looked at her, you know, in a way that she knew I was really interested. Later in the evening, we were all going to go outside to watch the fireworks. She and I reached the door about the same time. She looked at me briefly and smiled. I smiled back and put my arm around her. We stood watching the fireworks. Everything was going fine—and suddenly she took my arm from around her and says "Please" and then walks away. She then proceeds to tell several of the other women I was groping her. I swear I didn't do a thing other than hold her tight and look at her.

Regardless of the George's *intentions*, apparently his *actions* were interpreted by the woman as intrusive. Always remember, in dating, the other's interpretations matter, so be careful to send messages as unequivocal as possible. George wanted to insist all he did was use his eyes and hold her. Unfortunately for George, that can be enough. Human eyes carry a lot of clout—sometimes more than is intended. Touching, too, can be difficult. Genuinely friendly touches, those that characterize the behavior of "pals" are seldom offensive to others. On the other hand (pun intended), unwarranted touches to sensitive parts of the body, or those that send a too-intense message, alert the other to be on the lookout for sexual overtones.

The pitfalls of appearing promiscuous can be avoided even by the clumsiest of amateurs. Go ahead and try out different types of flirtations (saving any attempt at solicitous flirtations for moments of privacy when you are isolated with a consenting lover). In particular, remain mindful of the effect your eyes, body and touches can have on

Escalating Flirtation and Third Party Perception of Promiscuity

| | Innocent Flirtation | Serious Flirtation | Sexually Solicitous Flirtation |

% of Third party observers likely to view the flirtation as evidence of promiscuity: 0, 10, 20, 30, 40, 50, 60, 70, 80, 90

Note that very few people are likely to mistake an innocent flirtation as a sign of promiscuity. As the flirtation increases in intensity or otherwise changes character, it is taken to be a more serious flirtation while a slightly higher percentage of third party observers will infer promiscuity as the intent of a classic serious flirtation. Still, until the flirtation becomes sexually solicitous in character, the majority of third-party observers will assign no great significance to it. Finally, in the case of the most intense sexually solicitous flirtations, nearly all third-party observers are inclined to see this as some evidence of promiscuity, certainly of immediate sexual desire.

Summary

You waited a long time to enter the post-divorce lifestyle. There is no reason to rush into it head long or cower from entering it at all. In this chapter, I related the four most common pitfalls making post-divorce life unpleasant. By following the rules below you can probably avoid each of them.

1. Try not to use alcohol or any addictive drug for at least a year after the divorce or for as long as you remain haunted by any of the furies. You are especially vulnerable to addictive behavior at this stage in your life, so exercise extreme caution.

2. Commit yourself to your job and work hard at it. This is a great way to take your mind off unpleasant divorce-related thoughts. Hard work will also help your sense of achievement. DO NOT work excessively long hours. DO NOT work so hard you have no energy left for other activities.

3. DO NOT stay home night after night. DO go out with people at least two nights a week. Better yet, engage in some social activity with a member of the opposite sex at least once a week. Your first few attempts at dating may feel like a job-related task. That is okay. In a sense, it is a job. By forcing yourself to maintain a mixed social life, you build a sense of adventure and keep yourself open to new options.

4. DO NOT appear to be promiscuous. Be attentive to how you use your eyes.

    - If you are inclined to use metaphors such as "sizzling" to describe your mindset, you will probably court trouble more than people.

    - Be conscious of your body language.

    - Be careful about who you touch, how you touch them, and when you touch them. Be sensitive to their responses.

- Be discriminating with whom you flirt. Flirting is serious business. The more likely the person you are flirting with may see your action as issuing an invitation, the more careful you ought to be about to whom the invitation is extended, and the manner in which it is likely to be regarded.

- Feel comfortable about friendly handshakes, "pal-like" punches, pats on the back and arms.

5. When you are with a person on a date, it is not only good politics but also a matter of common courtesy to focus your attention on that person and not on a waiter, waitress, or some other person in the room. Not only your date but all other observers will appreciate your sense of decorum.

Avoid

- (For men) Hugs that are too tight. Do not place your hands too close to a woman's breasts or her bottom.

- (For women) Touching breasts or hips with deliberateness against the man. Avoid long touches to the front of a man's torso.

- (For both) Avoid hand grasps of other people's legs.

10

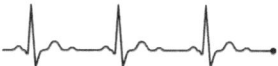

Parenting Through Divorce

Even though *Love Trauma* is intended as a book for the individual victim of divorce, like every other book, it has its limitations. One conspicuous limitation of *Love Trauma* is apparent: it has little to say to the divorcee with children. This is no mere oversight. As the father of four, I know only too well that addressing the continued familial relationships between children and parents burdens the divorcee with an additional set of problems: custody battles during divorce, managing a single parent family, the guilt of abandoning a family, fear of becoming Uncle Daddy or Aunt Mommy, all profoundly affect divorcees. Each profoundly affects the very being of everyone involved. These matters have each been the exclusive subject for numerous books over the past thirty years and well they should.

Love Trauma focuses on your immediate survival and subsequent romantic relations. I wish it could do more, but the book has distilled a massive amount of information. Perhaps with a good handbook for divorced parenting, you will find you can manage your world optimally well by referring to both.

In conclusion, I suggest a few criteria you might want to keep in mind when searching for that second, all-inclusive, handbook on divorced parenting. First, you should remember there are many types of love. The love of a spouse is quite different from the love of a parent. Each of these in turn is different from that of a parent for a child or a child for a parent. Furthermore, in each type of love, there exists a singularly unique variant within each pair of lovers. For example, if a mother has two daughters, Sarah and Martha, the mother's love for Sarah will be different from her love for Martha. This is not to say she will love one more than the other, it just means she will love each one differently.

Love of any kind is the most intimate of human relationships.

The uniqueness of each individual is a fundamental determinant in the course a love relationship takes. Sarah and Martha must be supposed to differ from one another in important ways; consequently, the relationship of love between Sarah and her mother will differ significantly from that between Martha and her mother.

Context is equally important for the expression of parental love. A child's love for a parent is affected by any hostility that exists between the parents. Assignment of custody affects future relationships between parent and child. Variance between the home environments offered by each parent influences the child's sense of belongingness and the parent's sense of responsibility. The dating activities of each parent also tend to confuse the child as to the nature of love and the enduringness of their own relationship to a given parent.

Social scientists have carried out numerous studies in recent years showing divorce is devastating to children. And divorce profoundly imperils the parent/child relationship. Parents have become increasingly aware of this fact and are taking the consequences of divorce on family life far more seriously than they did in the past. While there is much concern about these issues and much opinionated advice, there is little in the way of good, solid information. What information is available has not been collected and made available to consumers in a one easy to read volume. The need for such a volume is great.

Divorce-parenting is every bit as complicated and challenging as enduring a love trauma. If you are a divorced parent who has read this far, you can take comfort in the idea that at least now you have one very important area of your life under control. Having achieved this, even without additional advice on divorce-parenting, you may find you are parenting better as an indirect consequence of doing better in your social life.

As you bring each area of your life under control, your ability to negotiate the remaining problematic areas increases. As you come to understand the perplexities of a piece of life, you subsequently learn to manage it. This frees your deliberative resources for issues which continue to confuse and confound you. And the more you experience success in one domain, the self-esteem it creates often carries over to other areas as well giving you the confidence to address problems you previously feared were insurmountable. The divorcee who, with the assistance of this book, succeeds in his or her personal life will, I hope, experience an indirect benefit in parenting as well.

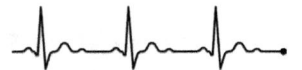

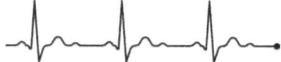

Epilogue — Who You Are

Divorce is part of your chronological past. You are single, but you don't know quite what to do about that. If this describes you, then read Part II again and meditate on those passages you most closely identify with. If divorce is now as much a part of your psychological past as your chronological past, then you can exploit fully the social advantages of single life described in my book, Love Drama: Romance, Delights and the Possibility of Subsequent Marriage.

Single life may again culminate in another marriage for some. Presumably, the prospects of another divorce never recede so far into the past the risk is felt as inconsequential. The next book explores prospects for a single life, marriage, potential spouses, and the sorts of things required to make the next relationship work. Again, study the spectrum below. If you find you are somewhere on it DO NOT move on to Book 2! People who attempt to rush through divorce to arrive at the best the hereafter has to offer only confound themselves and repeat the mistakes of their past. Take your time. Be honest. Move ahead but only at a pace which is right for you.

PART II

"What's it all about…?"	Loneliness	Aloneness	Wonderment	Finding a Home	Pitfalls	On My Way	Social Life / Dating
· Here I am, alone and with no idea of what's ahead. · What can I make of my future? · What have I made of my past?	· It's scary to be off on one's own! · It's depressing. · Does anyone care what happens to me?	· Now that I'm getting to know me, I'm discovering I'm really quite a good sort. · I thoroughly enjoy being by myself.	· WOW! The world has a lot more interest to it than I ever expected. · Learning to explore.	· Just what kind of single am I? · Adopting a new social role.	· Booze and drugs are your enemy. · Work CAN suffocate you. · Don't die at home. · The fast life finishes too fast.	· Date · Think friendly. · Be productive. · You're a great person to spend a thoughtful evening with.	· Being single ain't so bad! · Where do I meet my kind of people? · How can I be sure members of the other sex will find me Interesting?

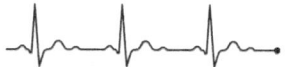

About the Author

Paul A. Wagner is a Ph.D., University of Missouri. He has taught courses in psychology, business management, philosophy, and education. He has held a number of senior level positions in national academic and scholarly organizations. He has also held positions on a number of Boards of Director in various organizations within the city of Houston and as Vice Chair of the City of Columbia's Human Rights Commission. He is a specialist in practical and applied ethics and moral theory. He himself has been a divorcee. He also has a long period of dating experiences going back to his class president days in college. He has written popular pieces on romance in the Austin American Statesman and the Dallas Morning News. He is the author of five books and over 100 publications ranging from philosophy and religion to the business of healthcare, probability, cognition, organizational development, learning theory, and the conditions for being a moral person. Once, as a result of volunteering by pushing a book cart around M.D. Anderson Cancer Center in Houston, he wrote a piece describing the romantic moments some patients experience as they cope with cancer while others realize they have no reliable companion at the end. He has had the opportunity to avail himself of the resources of a variety of social circles and in each he learned what he could about people's attitude towards marriage, divorce, dating, and responsibilities regarding child-rearing.

www.ingramcontent.com/pod-product-compliance
Lightning Source LLC
Chambersburg PA
CBHW021148080526
44588CB00008B/263